LAWYERS BROKEN BAD

LAWYERS BROKEN BAD

– ON LEGAL SYSTEM DYSFUNCTION IN THE USA AND SWITZERLAND –

introducing the *Lawyer Betrayal Syndrome*

Mark Inglin

Copyright © 2016 Mark Inglin
All rights reserved.

ISBN-13: 9781537661797
ISBN-10: 1537661795

*for Erich, my son
and for Celing Tang of Hong Kong, for inspiration*

*... and everywhere
the ceremony of innocence is drowned;
the best lack all conviction, while the worst
are full of passionate intensity.*

from The Second Coming, by W. B. Yeates

TABLE OF CONTENTS

Preface ································ix
Introduction ··························xiii

Part 1	**The Administration of Injustice** ··········· 1
	Legal Systems 1 and 2 ················· 4
	A System Unto Itself ·················· 14
	The Plea Bargain: a Good Solution ········ 19

Part 2	**Lawyer Advantage** ····················· 26
	Innocence as Crime ··················· 26
	The Courage to Defend ················ 33
	Phishermen and Phools ················ 37
	Phases of Lawyer Representation ········· 42
	Lawyer Tools for Betrayal ··············· 53
	Certain Lawyer Rewards················ 63

Part 3	**Client Burden** ························ 68
	The Power of Accusation ··············· 68
	But You Can Always Leave a Bad Lawyer! ··· 72
	The Psychology of Betrayal ············· 78

| | The Nervous System and Betrayal · · · · · · · · · 83 |
| | The *Lawyer Betrayal Syndrome* · · · · · · · · · · 87 |

Part 4	**Failures of Oversight** · · · · · · · · · · · · · · · · · · · 93
	Admitting Error · 102
	Police Crimes ·111
	Media and Bias ·115

| Part 5 | **Choosing a 'Good' Lawyer** · · · · · · · · · · · · · 125 |

Afterword · 131
Appendix · 135
Miscellaneous Examples of Legal System Dysfunction · 135
Bibliography · 155
Books: · 155
About the author · 157

PREFACE

IN 2007, THE book *The Purpose Driven Life* sold 30 million copies, topping the *Wall Street Journal* and *Publishers Weekly* bestseller charts. I never made a purchase, but I did take note of the wide acclaim that surrounded the book. It was no surprise to me that there was universal hunger to find meaning in life. By 2007 I had already found my purpose; it began in an American courtroom years earlier. This book, and its exposition of how legal systems malfunction and do harm, is another step on the path of my life's purpose.

Years ago, I stood by powerless as my son's young life was rearranged to suit high-cost lawyers in a legal system that encouraged an agenda that no American would have recognized as legal. I remember asking myself, "Would a defense lawyer deliberately betray his own client and assist the prosecution at a trial? "No," I answered, "that would be impossible." The deliberate concealment of evidence by lawyers and police, intimidation of witnesses, falsification of court documents, improper jury selection, and the wholesale abandonment of principles of law and ethics subsequently resulted in the loss of a child. As a father, I will never forget that it was naïve trust in the legal system that led to harm to my only son. Providing an explanation of how lawyers defeat their own clients motivated me to write this book.

Throughout my encounters with the legal system a nagging question kept arising: Was my personal experience of violations of ethics and law in one legal jurisdiction, Milwaukee, USA, unique? Perhaps there was something unusual about me, a personal deficiency that made me the exception. Was I unworthy of defense? Or was it Milwaukee that was exceptional? Today I know that none of these is true.

Some time ago I heard a man who had been sexually abused by Catholic clergy express how relieved he was when that scandal emerged to public acknowledgement, other voices besides his finally being heard. The man had isolated himself in a state of shame and self-doubt due to lack of support. Like that man, it took time for me to recognize repeating patterns of general misconduct in the legal system, and to understand that I was not alone.

Since I told a personal story in an earlier book, *Beyond Outrage*, the question of whether I was unique has been resoundingly answered: No! I was not. Like the Catholic Church, the legal system also exploits isolation and an absence of cohesion among its victims to its advantage. This book emerges from a belief that there are many voices yet to be raised and heard on the betrayal of clients by their own lawyers.

This is my second book on the subject of a fundamentally dysfunctional legal system. When I began telling the story of what was essentially legally-sanctioned child abuse years ago in *Beyond Outrage*, it was angrily dismissed as an impossible fabrication. The characters named in the book were real people, powerful lawyers and judges not accustomed to having their misconduct exposed for review outside a tight, legal circle. Enraged when they saw their misbegotten deeds in print, they began a malicious campaign of personal attack on the internet, spreading seemingly credible, false and personally injurious information. In their eagerness to stop the flow of information they also trampled the First Amendment, awarding the largest penalty ever imposed against an author in the State of Wisconsin.

But things are changing. Today, numerous publications raise awareness of legal system wrongdoing and they are making a difference. This book adds to the growing list of complaints about a justice system that too often permits or intentionally encourages injustice.

The only thing worse than a dysfunctional legal system is a dysfunctional legal system that enjoys trust. The troubling issues raised in this book should be carefully examined before anyone signs on with a lawyer. I trust that the information and accounts presented here will serve to forewarn and forearm a potential legal client.

A copy of this book should accompany a client to a lawyer' office; it should be used to heighten the lawyer's awareness and concern for his client.

Mark Inglin
Zermatt, Switzerland, 11/2016

INTRODUCTION

OUR LEGAL SYSTEM comprises a select, powerful society, closed unto itself and sick within. From mounting reports of miscarriages of justice to violence by police on civilians, we hear of daily tragedies of human sacrifice on the altar of sloppy legal work, incompetence and, not infrequently, outright malfeasance– all protected within a powerful, legal framework.

While in the past the issue of corruption in the legal system was often couched in terms of a few 'bad apples,' it seems more the case today that bad apples predominate and that few, if any, good apples stand up to them. When I observed similar, poor conduct in legal systems in other countries and cultures, however, I had to conclude that the problems we see in the American justice system have roots deeper than regional legal culture; they are anchored in the human psyche and arise from environments that tolerate corruption. The prevailing myth in a country like Switzerland, for example, is that the alpine democracy does not suffer the 'American disease.' It surely does; the disease is human, not American.

As I wrote this book a question arose that demanded an answer and that deserves pondering by a reader: where do anecdotes– such as presented here– end, and where does general truth begin? I recognized the limited validity of poet William Blake's criticism that "To generalize is to be an idiot. To particularize is the lone distinction of merit." Yet generalization is instinctive and has practical benefit when anecdotes turn out to be predictive of general behavior often enough. For example, not long ago the average person saw little reason to question the official word of police following a deadly shooting. Information emerging from video recordings, however, has changed our perceptions. How often do police avoid truth in their official records? We do not know, but more people are asking questions.

The issue of how much credence to pay to an anecdote is one of statistics. However, the legal system guards many of its secrets from statistical analysis. Lawyers can betray clients, but how often do they? Status quo bias can skew the legal system away from justice, but how often does it? What happens in the privacy of a lawyer's office is difficult to record and prove, at least in a way that will matter within the legal system.

Statistics are lacking in the case of most forms of unethical lawyer conduct. We are thus forced to extrapolate from reported bad behavior that appears anecdotal in isolation, but that repeats too often to remain anecdotal. The lack of formal statistics not withstanding, this book argues that 'profiling,' or extrapolating from known qualities, such as practiced by the FBI, can prove useful when an individual identifies himself as a 'criminal defense lawyer.'

In contrast to Blake's quote, there is a different saying in the biological sciences: one example of a phenomenon constitutes a curiosity, two examples make a principle. I have witnessed far more than two examples of repeating bad lawyer behavior over many years, cultures apart. The patterns of behavior that I observed followed from the same, general environment of an imbalance of power quite unique to a legal system.

The legal environment also makes it possible for a lawyer to impede the flow of truthful information about lawyer activities with a client. We should not expect lawyers to help compile statistics on how often they betray their own clients rather than choosing a harder road to justice.

The author's personal encounters with legal wrongdoing, repeated and viewed alongside so many similar experiences reported in general media, provided insight and bolstered my courage to come forth here. It was the patterns of wrongdoing at multiple levels that caught my attention and fascinated me. I felt that describing these patterns for legal clients could help correct the power imbalance that exists between a lawyer and his client. This imbalance in the lawyer-client relationship is the basis for the problem of lawyers betraying their own clients.

Attributing dysfunction to the overall legal system is a facile activity; claiming that only a few bad apples are responsible ignores its prevalence. Legal system corruption, this book argues, is common and centers in a lawyer's office in a fundamental distortion that results from the client's personal need for defense, which causes him to expose vulnerabilities and dependence on the lawyer, and the seduction of the lawyer by his relative power. At the same time, the theoretical safeguards to the abuse of his power– appeals, professional oversight boards, local media– largely fail in typical cases.

To be sure, there are also destructive imbalances in power between the overall legal system and the solitary defense lawyer. These filter down to the lawyer and, from him, to the client whom he intends to defend, but who is also the 'weakest link' in the chain of authority. Although it may be a disagreeable task for a client in need of defense, he must understand and confront the limitations to his lawyer's willingness to provide the most vigorous defense.

This work illustrates how activities in a bad lawyer's office have far less to do with law than with psychology– that is, raw, diabolical, coercive psychological manipulation of a client. Pressures for personal gain and survival within the competitive legal system lead lawyers to betray clients whom they have promised to defend. What happens behind the closed door of a lawyer's office is critical to understanding why our justice system fails. The exercise of lawyer strategy, the sacred ground onto which laymen are advised not to tread, is often the excuse for lawyers to feign legal action but then to fail in providing proper defense. Dark arts are practiced instead, delivering, among others, unjust plea bargain settlements.

Failure by a lawyer to defend a client vigorously in violation of his mandate and counter to expectations creates an environment that can readily undermine a client's mental health. The *Lawyer Betrayal Syndrome*, introduced for the first time in this book, explains the psychological symptoms of clients who suffer the consequences of betrayal by their own defense lawyers. The symptoms are listed and their cause is explained here. Similar to the Stockholm Syndrome, the *Lawyer Betrayal Syndrome* results from an imbalance of power between a betraying lawyer and his victim, the client. The repeat financial and career 'success' of lawyer betrayal, in turn, reinforces the wider use of betrayal in the legal community, thereby creating an expanding environment for the *Lawyer Betrayal Syndrome* through a positive feedback loop.

Throughout this book I provide examples that have been gathered from twenty years of examining the legal system. My encounters, coupled to the experiences of many others and those reported by reliable media, led to this book. The sources included *The New Yorker*, the *New York Times*, *The Atlantic*, *The Huffington Post*, National Public Radio, PBS Frontline, TED Talks and, in particular, *The Marshall Project*, which provides in-depth coverage of issues involving the criminal justice system and stories of personal injustice.

This work is not scholarly in the sense of extensive footnotes or citations. Although it relays many anonymous experiences, their general validity can be established readily by examining existing legal environments through an internet search of the topics of false confessions, ineffective assistance of counsel, wrongful imprisonment, wrongful convictions, lawyer and police misconduct, DNA exonerations, legal abuse, the Innocence Project and many more.

While the topics covered here are not arcane– many have been widely reported, usually in cases of gross legal system failures that became high profile only years later– what caught my attention in mainstream reports of legal system wrongdoing was the absence of insight into the formative encounters between defense lawyers and their clients. While legal system failures are currently receiving ample exposure, there is far less exposure of failures in lawyer-client relationships. One explanation for this absence is obvious– the private, confidential nature of the lawyer-client interaction. The *Lawyer Betrayal Syndrome*, however, also plays a prominent role in concealing how lawyers deceive clients: betrayed clients struggle emotionally with exposing their lawyers and holding them accountable.

The legal system corruption that I observed and reconciled with broader media reports, along with the ubiquitous refusal within the legal system to admit even the most egregious errors, leads to the conclusion that there are two, distinct legal systems. I call these theoretical Legal System 1 and practical Legal System 2. In this book I provide examples of problems created by Legal System 2 and why it overwhelms and replaces Legal System 1 so often and so readily.

This book has several self-imposed, intentional limitations. First, it concerns *only* bad lawyers and bad lawyering. Indeed, what is written here is highly unfair to good lawyers. I just wish that I had run into one to apologize in advance for the unfairness. A client may expect and then receive the best of legal representation and justice in the legal system, but understanding what can go wrong should make a favorable outcome more likely for any client.

Another important limitation here is that I refer solely to criminal defense lawyers who represent clients who wish to claim innocence to a criminal charge. This book is not about clients who wish to plead guilty and look forward to mitigating their offenses through a plea bargain or settlement. It also does not concern corporate lawyers, real estate lawyers, patent lawyers, lawyers who do wills and estates etc., most of whom work in environments that typically do not include the life-altering threats and fears that exist in the criminal justice system.

While personal legal experience may be alien to many readers, most of us are familiar with the pain caused by betrayal and deceit in everyday life. A while ago, an acquaintance lamented to me about a partner who had betrayed her trust and left her in a stitch. She wondered why the offender could not sense the pain caused by his betrayal. "Why could he not see the cruelty of his offense?" I offered the explanation that this is common and not a great concern to the other side. There is a vast difference in awareness between being the axe and being the tree– the axe forgets, the tree remembers.

While preparing this book I visited a lawyer's office near my home in Zermatt, Switzerland. I wanted to have first use of the term *Lawyer Betrayal Syndrome* notarized for copyright purposes. The lawyer nervously indicated that he had a meeting to go to but, as he was about to affix his seal, he took note for the first time of the subject headline, which in German was *Anwalt-Betrug-Syndrom (Lawyer Betrayal Syndrome)*. Ignoring the urgency of his meeting, he began to read the document intently, then gazed at me with a look of sobriety.

"This is harsh," he observed.

He spoke seriously and respectfully and, entirely unsolicited, he began to explain himself and his actions as a lawyer. It was a confirmation of off-the-record accountability that I had witnessed at other times from lawyers. What lawyers do to clients is often regretted by lawyers as much as it is by clients. I felt as if I had just shown a magician how he performs his most guarded magic trick. This book is about arousing such awareness. It is written for the trees; hopefully it will also cause the axe to reconsider.

PART 1

THE ADMINISTRATION OF INJUSTICE

IN "THE UNTOUCHABLES: America's Misbehaving Prosecutors and the System that Protects Them," Radley Balko of the *Huffington Post* relates the story of John Thompson, who was wrongly convicted twice in separate cases for carjacking and murder. He was imprisoned for eighteen years at the Louisiana State Penitentiary and spent fourteen years on death row. His death warrant became official eight times. He was weeks from execution when he was finally cleared by evidence that prosecutors concealed for years.

"In the end, there was no accountability," Balko explained. "Thompson's case produced a surfeit of prosecutorial malfeasance, from incompetence to poor training, a culture of conviction that included both willfully ignoring evidence that could have led to his exoneration to blatantly withholding it."

Thompson, after his release, said, "This isn't about bad men– though they were most assuredly bad men– it's about a system that is void of integrity. Mistakes can happen. But if you don't do anything to stop them from happening again, you can't keep calling them mistakes."

Bryan Stevenson, Professor of Clinical Law at New York University School of Law, pointed out in a *TED talk* that the rate of error on death row is one in nine. That is, one in nine individuals on death row was there by error and has been exonerated. This is mostly due, he explained, to overzealous prosecutors who are more concerned with advancing their legal careers than administering justice; rules are simply ignored.

In a Harvard Law School report titled "America's Top Five Deadliest Prosecutors," researchers found that prosecutors who seek the death penalty more frequently than their peers have alarmingly high rates of personal misconduct. The report identifies five head prosecutors who, together, were responsible for 440 death sentences, equivalent to approximately 15 percent of the current U.S. death row population. According to the report:

> Their overzealous pursuit of the death penalty does not accurately reflect America's growing skepticism of the death penalty, nor is it representative of local constituencies that are more attached to the death penalty. It better reflects the lack of meaningful controls on prosecutorial discretion and a lack of consequences for their illegal or unethical behavior.

The report also found that when four of these prosecutors retired, death sentences declined dramatically in their jurisdictions, a trend that researchers say shows that individual personalities drove the death sentencing rates, and not any commitment to capital punishment by local citizens. Eight people sentenced to die under district attorneys on the list were later exonerated and released from death row.

How is it possible that prosecutors who advocate for the ultimate punishment, the death of defendants, can themselves not be held accountable by the legal system for their misconduct? The legal safeguards associated with putting a person to death are theoretically in full effect to rule out error. If a cavalier attitude displays itself through individual misconduct in death penalty cases, what can we expect at lower levels, in routine cases?

Prosecutors possess what they themselves admit are unaccountable powers, powers vested by an institution that can provoke fear to a degree greater than found almost anywhere else, except possibly organized crime. Unfortunately, lack of accountability is widespread in the legal system– not just for prosecutors and not just in relation to death penalty cases. Lack of accountability gets worse down the line, where statistics are far less likely to be kept and unethical or illegal conduct is far less likely to emerge in any report.

Like overzealous prosecutors, ordinary lawyers in ordinary cases operate with a different set of rules from that put forth for public consumption. An overall lack of accountability in the legal system leads to the freedom for prosecutors and for lawyers to apply more than one set of rules: different rules applied to different people is a hallmark of corruption.

A great irony in the legal system is that, due to widespread lack of accountability, wrongdoing by members of the legal profession need not be defined as crime, while any collusion by members of the legal system to hide internal wrongdoing– a common occurrence– need not be defined as organized crime. Instead, wrongdoing is passed up the line, along to the next legal level of hoped-for accountability. Victims of legal system wrongdoing are instructed to "appeal," which then conveniently renders earlier activities that were incompetent, negligent, unethical or illegal activities on the part of lawyers merely a part of the 'legal' process. To hold the legal system itself responsible for any wrongdoing, however, is practically meaningless; only by holding individuals accountable for individual acts within the legal system will the legal system be forced to clean itself up.

In Switzerland, a court of first instance violated ethical and legal rules to an extent practically impossible to describe as unintentional. A district attorney's office later explained that the misconduct should not be reported openly, as the "next court" would render a finding in the appeal. "Let's first see how they rule," it was strongly suggested. Only in the legal system, in both the USA and in Switzerland, can misconduct at lower levels be concealed and transferred in the veneer of legality as colleagues up the line are asked to find colleagues down the line culpable.

LEGAL SYSTEMS 1 AND 2

Popular culture upholds an image of our legal system as one that is fair, impartial, and effective at providing justice. In such a legal system, the one we call Legal System 1 here, lawyers defend innocent clients vigorously, judges are cautious about their judgments, police present all of the available evidence, and recourse is provided in the form of appeals and oversight for clients treated unfairly. This is the legal system that we hear about in the media, books, and from Hollywood, the one that most of us imagine that we will have when we, or our friends or loved ones, wind up in legal trouble.

In reality, the law as it is often practiced is completely different from the law as presented to the public. We will call the usurper the practical Legal System 2. In Legal System 2 the rules are fuzzy, flexible and influenced by politics, power, and status quo bias. Its practitioners are ruthlessly Darwinian, but instead of physical competition for the survival of the fittest, they engage in concealed, subtle competition between human nervous systems in an unfair, highly power-imbalanced battle of minds.

Legal System 1 holds, for example, that prosecuting attorneys must play fair, provide the defense with exculpatory evidence and, of course, tell the truth. In Legal System 2, prosecutors focus on winning, not on justice or truth. Prosecutors and lawyers are not held to standards that require truthfulness. The gap between what is said (Legal System 1) and what is done (Legal System 2) creates a system of corruption that ruins lives, wastes scarce resources and permits actual lawbreakers to escape justice.

Legal System 2 has little to do with law, ethics, truth or justice. It not only tolerates and makes use of two different sets of rules to deceive, but it lends to the deceit respect and claims that special rules are necessary and justified for legal practitioners. Years ago, I had my first taste of how Legal System 1 bows to more primitive motives, as I watched an experienced lawyer in his first encounter in the courtroom with his opponent. His approach surprised me then; he was openly insulting and aggressive, which I noticed took the other lawyer's client aback. When asked by his client why he had acted in that seemingly unnecessary manner, this normally affable, generally polite lawyer explained that the courtroom environment made it necessary to "establish my dominance right from the start." Dominance, not the facts, would impress the judge and push back the other lawyer. He explained that this made winning the case more likely.

While the provision of evidence is the absolute cornerstone to the concept of justice in Legal System 1, in Legal System 2 evidence is frequently and readily manipulated or entirely excluded from consideration at the discretion of legal system players who have the power to do so. Reports can be altered, transcripts deleted, and witnesses coerced, all without accountability.

The public is led to believe that evidence presented in court and as reported in media represents the actual evidence available in a case. The universal impression that evidence is what drives a legal outcome misdirects a real understanding of how the legal system works. In fact, Legal System 2 permits the exclusion or alteration of evidence that is not 'clean.' Evidence that is clean has been laundered and casts no negative light on any legal system player. Repackaging evidence for a predetermined result and to spare embarrassment is understood as a major goal by Legal System 2, ensuring that outcomes favor the legal system as a whole, not the client or justice.

In a felony case in Wisconsin that depended on the results of a court-ordered psychological examination, a lawyer altered the psychological report to state the opposite of the original report. A summary of the false report was then provided to a federal judge, who ruled based on the false documentation. The misconduct was subsequently hidden, the offending lawyer protected. When informed, the federal judge claimed he had no jurisdiction and refused to consider the matter further.

In a case in Switzerland, a defense lawyer concealed evidence of wrongdoing by a university and a law professor, evidence vital to a criminal exoneration. When the client insisted on the presentation of the evidence, the lawyer refused to continue his representation. Protecting the university and the status quo, the judge in the case refused to hold the lawyer accountable for his violation of professional duty. The client hired another lawyer, but the judge then refused to grant adequate trial preparation time. The defendant was forced to go to trial without legal counsel. At trial, the judge acted on behalf of the prosecution, which had failed to appear. Protected from accountability, even the accusers failed to appear. Evidence aplenty was available, but it never saw the light of day, as local media turned a blind eye.

What we consider hard, incontrovertible evidence is actually highly malleable when manipulated within Legal System 2.

MARK INGLIN

In a case in Wisconsin, evidence was concealed to protect a police detective who himself had concealed exculpatory evidence in a child abuse case in his desk drawer for years following a trial that returned a child to his abuser. Later, that detective became a police chief. His career was built on the foundation of a defense lawyer who had betrayed his own client, a corrupt prosecutor who protected the police, and a complicit appellate lawyer. All had worked in concert to spare the legal system, deliberately turning a blind eye to misconduct by colleagues

With evidence sidelined, judgments can be reached based on intuition, prejudice, politics and past experiences instead of facts. For example, prejudices about what someone looks or acts like when lying lead people to believe incorrectly that a person has lied, possibly based on a facial tic or other mannerism. Many similar assumptions based on intuition have been proven false when tested. But the deliberate exploitation of these false assumptions continues to put the wrong people in prison or on death row. Superstitions are as rampant among judges, prosecutors and lawyers as they are among tarot card readers or even baseball players. As justification for the continuation of false assumptions in light of incontrovertible scientific evidence, we are instructed that the legal system is 'conservative' and 'cautious,' with 'tradition' a key virtue.

In Legal System 2, the application of intuition and "experience" permits what lawyers refer to as 'paternalism' to determine outcomes. Paternalism allows lawyers and judges to cut corners to save time and taxpayer money. Cutting corners means not providing the safeguards guaranteed by Legal System 1. Paternalism is usually applied when legal clients have little influence, knowledge of the law or money in a community. Due process, the vital ingredient to Legal System 1, becomes an impractical restriction. Lawyers and judges 'size up' a person and rely on 'experience.'

A fundamental problem in striving for justice using Legal System 1 is that a strong bias due to human nature exists in favor of Legal System 2. Legal System 1 requires thought, effort, hard work and, not infrequently, the emotional discomfort of tough decisions by those in power. Legal System 2 is the easier path: a few, stiff drinks with the boys at the club after work. Legal System 1 is the gym, a heart-smart dinner and helping the children with their math problems before bed.

Professionals in the legal system fully understand that perceptions are influenced by preexisting biases and psychological influences. Legal System 2 and paternalism make use of common prejudices and perceptions. For example, something as simple as the placement of a recording camera in an interrogation room has been shown to influence whether a confession is considered to be coerced. When observers watch a recording with the camera positioned behind an interrogating detective, they are far more likely to find that a confession was voluntary. If they watch the interactions from the perspective of the suspect, they are more likely to think it was coerced. As reported by *The Economist* magazine, it has also been shown that decisions by judges are influenced by whether those decisions are made before or after lunch, blood glucose levels being the determining factor!

Data show that matches involving fingerprints and DNA are significantly more likely when a forensic expert is aware that the sample comes from someone accused of a crime by the police. The way that a question is asked can guide a jury to reach desired conclusions. Memories have been shown to be readily altered by the careful selection of words used by a lawyer or police to question a witness. Memories can be corrupted and undermined, for example by forced, repeated recall of a memory coupled with a favored interpretation of events. Putting forth false evidence or downplaying the seriousness of an offense can lead people to confess to crimes of the worst sort that they did not commit. Suggestibility under stress is a real phenomenon, but one that is difficult to comprehend by individuals not actually placed under the type of stress that provokes it.

Even DNA evidence, once thought to be unassailable, has been shown to be fallible due to poor crime lab techniques and prosecution bias. As reported in the *Houston Chronicle*, a study of the Houston Police Department Crime Laboratory, among the largest public forensic centers in Texas and handling DNA evidence from at least 500 cases a year, found that Houston police technicians were routinely misinterpreting even the most basic samples.

Not long ago the FBI, the premier law enforcement agency in the USA, admitted publically that its laboratories and analysts had been providing flawed testimony for decades, impacting thousands of cases that included death penalty cases. Of 268 trials, the FBI admitted that an astonishing 257 (ninety-six percent) of those trials included tainted evidence that overwhelmingly favored the prosecution. Defendants were sentenced to prison and put to death based, in part, on flawed evidence.

All of the above doubts about objectivity not withstanding, we still see that interpretations of evidence are nevertheless routinely put forth at trials by declared experts with unwarranted confidence. Aside from DNA when handled properly, there are no other forms of evidence, such as fingerprints, bite marks, patterns in suspected arson, etc., that are unambiguous and universally agreed on. Despite the uncertainties, unjustified interpretations are permitted to prosecute defendants in a system where science is diminished by shoddy methods, unwarranted claims and legal superstitions. The poor results of supposed evidence are then codified by overzealous prosecutors and passively accepted by lawyers who fail to fight hard against the system on behalf of their clients.

Through an understanding of human psychology and neuroscience, we now see numerous areas in which common but incorrect assumptions and extraneous influences produce distortions throughout the legal system. A willingness to accept the results of neuroscience research could vastly improve the justice system. Much of this information remains remote to the public and is blocked from meaningful application. For example, we know with certainty today, through direct anatomical evidence, that the brains of adolescents are not fully developed in the region of the brain that controls impulses, behavior and judgment. Yet courts transfer adolescents to adult courts based on the perception of the seriousness of the crime, not on the mental capacity of the individual. Such considerations satisfy political needs, not Legal System 1. Unfortunately, attempts to bring rationality to law through neuroscience are heavily impeded by the legal system; restricting the application of false perceptions or manipulative and ethically or legally questionable tactics meets stiff resistance from the more influential Legal System 2.

Were it to admit to its errors, it is doubtful that there is any other institution or social organization with the potential to fuel as much anger, outrage and anguish as the legal system. That fact– the gravity of the profound changes brought to lives by errors within the legal system– may explain the powerful, collective resistance that we see from the legal system toward better means to determine truth, or the delays or prevention of disclosures of legal system wrongdoing. The legal system as such, of course, never makes any mistakes. It is individuals within the legal system who make mistakes. Those individuals, however, have intense, powerful working relationships within the legal system. The legal system is excellent at preventing the disclosure of wrongdoing and protecting its wrongdoers from responsibility.

One of the most serious violations that can be committed by any prosecutor is to withhold evidence that could help a defendant prove innocence or obtain a reduced sentence. This practice, however, is so widespread now that a federal judge, Alex Kozinsky, called it an "epidemic." Because prosecutor actions are, for all practical purposes, uncontestable, self-restraint for the sake of fairness and justice is trumped by the seduction of victory and career advancement. Racking up convictions translates into promotions for prosecutors and high-paying jobs later with prestigious law firms. Rules are broken or ignored, followed by effective denial. The *New York Times* editorial board drew attention to this by lamenting:

> In the end, one of the most powerful positions in public service– a position that carries with it the authority not only to ruin lives, but in many cases the power to end them– is one of the positions most shielded from liability and accountability. And the freedom to push ahead free of consequences has created a zealous conviction culture.

The solution to this problem, the editorial board offers, is to call on the Feds for oversight. Of course, many district attorneys' offices will resist monitoring by the federal government. They argue that self-regulation and sanctions by state regulatory authorities are adequate to prevent professional wrongdoing. In practice, studies show that professional misconduct by prosecutors is rarely brought to light or punished. Even a prosecutor who intentionally submits false evidence in a case that results in the wrongful conviction, or in the execution of an innocent person, cannot be held personally responsible.

Paradoxically, it is prosecutors who insist most intensely on punishment for wrongdoers. 'If bad behavior isn't punished, you should expect repeat bad behavior,' they explain with righteous logic regarding those convicted. Why does this supposed truism not then apply to prosecutors themselves? The idea that a group of people who have attended law school should be less prone to temptation and live lives of higher integrity than people in other professions is absurd. What is not absurd, because it is real, accepted and openly practiced, is that their power to exempt themselves from responsibility and punishment contributes heavily to Legal System 2.

When rewards for misconduct exceed those of lawful action, there can be little wonder when prosecutorial and law enforcement misconduct become rampant. There is no more effective way to reinforce bad behavior than to repeatedly allow it to enjoy financial and professional success. In the current system, wrongdoing by prosecutors, police and lawyers is accepted, even by the defense lawyer who has been hired specifically to expose that wrongdoing to the benefit of his client.

A SYSTEM UNTO ITSELF

Corruption can enter into any system that combines human nature, power imbalance, fear and neediness together with limited transparency and minimal public interest. These elements are abundant in our legal system. They create the conditions favorable for both lawyers and prosecutors to push aside the concerns of clients/defendants for their own careers, and to protect the status quo. As one example, this author's previous book *Beyond Outrage* revealed extensive evidence of the intimidation of witnesses, flawed jury selection, concealment of exculpatory evidence by lawyers and police, and a prosecutor who deliberately lied to a jury concerning court records and legal history. In depositions, this author was actively prevented from providing evidence in a libel case pertaining to essays, including threats by my own lawyer to prevent further publications. Ultimately, a default judgment that amounted to over one million dollars was imposed while I was out of the country, the largest amount ever awarded against an author in the State of Wisconsin. Lawyers who would normally have defended freedom of speech vigorously refused to do so in this case. Proper defense would have required implicating local legal players in serious, career-altering wrongdoing. Lawyers of the necessary caliber to meet such circumstances head-on are hard to find.

Among the factors that promote serious corruption in our criminal justice system, and that allow lawyers to rationalize the unethical manipulation of their clients, is the lack of resources in the legal system. In an article in the *New York Times* titled "Go to Trial, Crash the Justice System," law professor Michelle Alexander explains that, among its other serious problems, the American legal system has nowhere near the capacity required to handle its obligations, were every individual accused of a crime to insist on their constitutional right to a trial. The courtrooms, the judges, the public defenders and the funding are woefully lacking.

"The truth is that government officials have deliberately engineered the system to ensure that the jury trial system established by the Constitution is seldom used," explained Timothy Lynch, director of the Criminal Justice Project at the Cato Institute. Trials, as we shall see, can actually be dangerous venues not just for defendants, but also for lawyers, judges and for Legal System 2.

A lack of resources plays a large role as an excuse that encourages lawyers to view the manipulation and coercion of their own clients as unavoidable legal requirements. They become the tools to avoid trials that the system is ill equipped to handle and does not welcome. Handily, avoiding trials also has the benefit of concealing any possible earlier wrongdoing by the local power structure. Self-interest among legal players, all with a measure of power greater than the average legal client, is what moves the system in a direction that favors the system.

In a criminal justice case in Wisconsin involving a defendant charged with a third-degree felony, the defense lawyer and the judge engaged in extensive efforts to prevent the defendant from going to trial by threatening him with a whopping twenty years in a hard-time prison. These efforts included shouting and bouts of anger by the judge when the client continued to insist on innocence and his desire for a trial.

Both the judge and defense lawyer came to actively resent the unyielding defendant. The sentence finally imposed was one year of work release; total time served was nine months. In open court the judge mused audibly that he should "... probably avoid punishing the defendant for insisting on his right to a trial, costing my time and the county money." The judge's voice allowed no mistaking his resentment that an ordinary citizen had made his way to a trial against his wishes.

A client who is innocent can represent an annoyance and a conflict to a lawyer. He has to consider the reaction of an influential figure in his professional life, the judge, to one more demand on his time. The judge is like the holder of five World Series tickets who has six friends. The friend who advises that he does not care for baseball makes the ticket holder's life much easier. A defendant who insists on proving innocence has the lawyer demanding a ticket to an important event, except that there would be far more than six competitors for those tickets.

The lawyer who attempts to bring too many cases into a judge's courtroom will be viewed as disrespecting the needs of the system and the needs of other lawyers in the community hierarchy. He may not be welcome, for example, on a judge's court calendar. Scheduling and day-to-day legal operations that allow a lawyer to make a living suddenly become more difficult. And there isn't a thing that the lawyer can do about it, except to get in line with the program.

A conscientious lawyer can unleash subtle disdain or a hell-storm of antipathy from his legal community by exposing wrongdoing by local legal players, or by defending a client too vigorously when that client's defense depends on exposing legal system failures. I knew a lawyer in New Zealand who, at the start of any criminal representation, ranked phone calls made to his office so as to determine a new client's influence in the community and, consequently, the level of respect, concern and defense accorded to him. Guilt or innocence and the law were an afterthought. If the client received little support, had little influence or power in the community, and therefore was of no media interest, the incentive to defend that client diminished.

If defense requires implicating local police, lawyers, judges, politicians or other, well-connected individuals in the community in wrongdoing, suddenly a lawyer faces a dilemma. He will receive phone calls from people in his professional circle; he will feel pressure to avoid putting forth evidence to defend his client.

Of course, no lawyer wishes to be responsible for "crashing the legal system" that he depends on to make a living. Aside from the many hours of preparatory work and the risk of loss at trial, the lawyer who insists on granting his clients trials will eventually be viewed as a troublemaker or nuisance, as out of sync with the operation of the legal system as his insistent client. In his legal community, that lawyer can come to be viewed as unable or unwilling to apply the necessary pressure to *bring his client under control,* a condition eagerly sought after a retainer has been paid. That lawyer will be seen as too soft to practice law as it needs to be practiced in the current legal system. The lawyer faces a practical choice: anger the client or anger his colleagues.

THE PLEA BARGAIN: A GOOD SOLUTION

On his cable television show Bill Maher, a well-known American political commentator and comedian, referred to what he called the single most important statistic that characterizes today's criminal justice system in the United States: ninety-five percent of criminal cases never go to trial; they are settled instead by plea bargaining. The coercion of legal clients by their own defense lawyers, he suggested, dominates the American system of justice. Rousing applause from the audience implied that what was once considered arcane information has filtered down to common perception and concern.

The solution to the lack of legal resources, fear of negative repercussions from influential community or legal system members, professional disadvantage and too much hard work is readily at hand: the plea bargain settlement. Simply stated, a plea bargain has a defendant relinquish a claim of innocence and the right to a trial in exchange for an admission of guilt and lesser punishment. The temptation to accept a plea bargain is that the client can avoid potential punishment that is far worse if he goes to trial and loses. Plea bargaining relieves an overburdened legal system, but it is also highly expedient for more nefarious purposes. In a corrupt legal system, the plea bargain has become the bad lawyer's ticket to success and a goal in itself.

A lawyer feels both emotional and professional pressure if a trial is to be held to prove his client innocent. If he does not win, and the best of efforts can obviously fail for countless reasons, he must continue his career knowing that he was inadequate to the task and that he possibly sent an innocent person to prison or worse. A loss with such high stakes is not easy to confront or live with. Moreover, a loss at trial will count negatively on a professional record. This is far worse for a lawyer than a settlement, which is neutral or quite often viewed as success. Few people will know if a client was innocent and wished to defend that innocence at a trial. If the client was innocent, it is reasoned, then why did he plea bargain? Surely that could not be the lawyer's fault. There must have been some level of client guilt involved.

With a plea bargain, the client is forced to assume the responsibility for his pleading, while at the same time any improper methods used to coerce that client to enter into a plea bargain will remain unexplored. Innocent clients who have plea bargained under pressure often have great difficulty explaining their reasoning afterwards, especially following betrayal by their lawyers.

An army veteran had engaged in a scheme that sold a service that, in some convoluted fashion, claimed that banks would be held responsible for bounced checks. He felt strongly that he had not violated the law knowingly and asked for a trial. The prosecution threatened the accused with 15 years in prison. His lawyer urged him to accept a six-year sentence in a plea bargain. He agreed. But in prison not a day passed without his regret for having plea bargained rather than gone on to a trial, to tell his story. An intense feeling of having suffered a significant defeat followed him. "Why was I able to confront danger in battle with little fear of death," he asked himself, "yet I capitulated so easily to the prosecutor's threat, which didn't compare, really?"

Given the risks involved for a lawyer who goes to a trial, it should not be a surprise that a client who insists on having a trial to prove innocence will cause unease or even a punitive reaction from his lawyer and/or the judge. With intense client insistence, the lawyer and the judge might well wish to *teach the nuisance a lesson*. After all, if one client can 'abuse' the system by insisting on a trial, others may be tempted to try the same strategy. It is therefore important for a lawyer to assume control of a client as soon as possible and to work toward abandoning any ideas of going to a trial.

The justice system today has evolved to a point at which going to trial is viewed by lawyers as a major failure, the failure to bring a client under control. Prominent in any lawyers' mind therefore is: How do I impose control over my client?

A prominent criminal defense lawyer, who was once acclaimed in Time magazine for his legal skills, preferred to impose control over a client at the time of his release on bail. He induced psychological stress in his client by informing him that his release from jail was imminent, proclaiming the date and the hour, but then intentionally dashing the client's eagerly-contemplated expectations not once but repeatedly. As highlighted later in this book, raising and dashing expectations is an important lawyer tool and can be used effectively to weaken possible client resistance to lawyer demands.

Legal System 1 does not provide instructions to a lawyer on how to impose control over his own client; the psychology of coercion and how best to attain the plea bargain arise from word of mouth, lawyer to lawyer, and experience gained in Legal System 2.

Convincing a client to accept a plea bargain is therefore easier and also beneficial to a lawyer's career. One thing is certain: the record will never state, 'The client desperately wanted to go to trial to prove his innocence, but his lawyer coerced him to admit guilt so that the lawyer wouldn't have to risk losing at trial, annoying a judge or disrupting his work environment.'

While some defendants hold fast to their insistence on their innocence, there are many who will readily agree to a plea bargain– like the ex-soldier above– even if they did not commit a crime. They do this for a reason that is poorly understood. They plea bargain in order to relieve the emotional burden that results from the punitive nature of the legal system. The concept of being innocent until proven guilty has no practical meaning. The justice system imposes burdens right from the start of a criminal charge. Sadly, limbo in a punitive legal system that deliberately causes stress is worse for some people than a quick guilty plea with a defined outcome in sight.

Whether ethical or not, whether admitted or not, defense lawyers, judges and prosecutors do collude to frighten defendants into plea bargaining. The individual who resists such an effort can trigger reactions from any or all of the legal players involved in his case. The word "no" spoken to power– a lawyer, a prosecutor or a judge– is rarely a means to generate warmth of feelings, but often a reason for resentment and retribution.

Even though direct evidence of coercion of their own clients by defense lawyers to achieve plea bargains is impossible to come by, it is hard to arrive at any other explanation for the ninety-five percent plea bargain statistic. The plea bargaining process is a black box overall in terms of generating statistics, and it is meant to be so: it allows the lawyer to define a legal outcome without a trial and without effective oversight of the methods used to achieve the plea bargain. Meaningless promises and outright deceit of a client can hardly be contested after a plea bargain agreement, due to the confidential nature of the lawyer-client interaction. No genuine pronouncement can then be made as to the performance of the lawyer. The only comparison that can be drawn, and the one that is boastfully drawn by the defense lawyer, is between the final result of the plea bargain versus the threat offered-up by the prosecution, not infrequently in coordination with improper complicity by the defense lawyer.

A lawyer in Wisconsin who was known as a plea bargain specialist employed shills– his secretary and a private investigator who worked for him– to hold ostensibly objective "pre-trial practice sessions" in his office. These practice sessions, clients were told, would prepare the client for trial– an entirely reasonable proposition. But the sessions were rigged; they were used to contrive reasons for a client to plea bargain.

The lawyer prepared questions that he would pose to a client who intended to go to trial rather than plea bargain. He then provided the shills with the appropriate answers and even suggested certain facial expressions, in order to convince the client that he would not be well received by a jury.

That same lawyer had permission from his favorite judge to schedule trial dates that were intentionally 'flexible.' Client and defense witnesses were subject to the stress of the anticipation of a supposedly fixed trial date, but the date was repeatedly and suddenly cancelled the day before, causing anger and turmoil. All of that stress can be avoided, a lawyer assures a client, if the client plea bargains.

As the courts have repeatedly upheld the rights of police and lawyers to effectively mislead suspects/clients, a lawyer is literally licensed to invoke client fear by lying, that is, by providing false, intentionally misleading information and other forms of deceit. What does it take to finally make someone accept a plea bargain? The threat of 20 years in prison? 30? 40? And who knows if the threatened amount of time in prison is a bluff or realistic? Any attempt to determine whether the lawyer abused his power in private with a client by providing false information and threats will be almost impossible to establish.

LAWYERS BROKEN BAD

There are criminal defense lawyers who spend their entire careers without going to trial to defend a client. These same lawyers will assure every client that a trial awaits them if they want one. This is one, important lawyer sales tactic. Such lawyers are surreptitious plea bargain specialists. A comparison might be made to a general medical practitioner who promises a patient that he will perform his heart bypass surgery– it's not going to happen. However, this false advertising is not professional folly in the legal system. The lawyer who is a plea bargain specialist almost always gets his way; he feels justifiably confident that he can change a client's mind. He knows how to manipulate a client psychologically, and he holds the power to do so. He knows of the impact of fear and the threat of loss on his client's psyche, and that *no one will stop him*. For such lawyers, manipulation or outright coercion are far easier than following the law.

PART 2

LAWYER ADVANTAGE

INNOCENCE AS CRIME

THERE CAN BE something quite annoying about a person who claims innocence. Perhaps it traces back to childhood. The authoritarian parent asked the child, 'Why did you allow yourself to get into that situation in the first place?' Innocence becomes associated with fear. Blaming the victim is an age-old but also effective remedy for an absence of courage to defend innocence, or an unwillingness to tolerate the psychic tension that arises from the circumstance of someone claiming innocence.

The act of claiming innocence to a crime conjures an image of the accused person actually having committed the crime. For example, claiming innocence to a charge of murder or rape invites consideration of the person doing precisely that. Could they have done that? A false accusation in some ways has the same effect as a valid accusation; it wipes away an unstained image forever, placing a seed of doubt in the minds of others.

Our legal system holds little or no respect for accused individuals who claim innocence. The saying "innocent until proven guilty" has become essentially meaningless. Proof of this can be seen in any county jail, for example by the third-world conditions that often exist, bad food intended as punishment, the poor health care that is provided or the limited access to family members when bail is unaffordable.

Claiming innocence is a great emotional and, in the legal system, financial burden. Proclaiming innocence is also an existential issue. There is the common fear of being innocent and yet not being believed. A state of innocence confronts a world in which its disbelief can easily be preferred for purely emotional reasons apart from any facts, as in seeing beautiful people as universally virtuous, while the less endowed are guilty. In Legal System 2, simple-minded intuition or prejudices are exploited by prosecutors as well as by defense lawyers, as long as they can lead to conviction or to a plea bargain.

Proclaiming innocence can literally force an individual to defend his existence as an individual, as his defense must project his own sense of worthiness as the individual. Proclaiming innocence can be especially difficult for an individual in cultures where social values and the group take priority over the individual. An accused individual must be able to proclaim his own, special nature even when accused by the all-powerful state. Once accused, a person must stand up alone and indeed take himself 'seriously.'

The bad lawyer not only lacks respect for innocence, but he sees it instead as a nuisance or a career threat most easily dealt with through a coerced confession and plea bargain.

There is an illustrative paradox that arises if we compare lawyer attitudes and passions in the defense of guilt to the defense of innocence. It is not uncommon to hear defense lawyers boast of their skills in setting a client free, perhaps on a legal technicality, while the lawyer himself and everyone else thought the client to be guilty of the crime as charged. It is as if the real test of lawyer manhood were not to be found in the defense of innocence, but rather in the exhibition of the skills to legally defy the legitimate strictures of society.

The above paradox represents a common, psychological twist. Due to their emotionally perverse working environment, with lies respected and truth reviled so often, defense lawyers evolve from admirable, early idealism to exhibit a disdain for innocence and open admiration for the deviant client who has defied the law. The bad lawyer preens on his successful defense of the outlaw. Just like any other environment, the legal environment, with its respect for Legal System 2 and all of its permissible shortcuts, nurtures and grows bad lawyers with bad principles.

Entirely legally in the defense of guilt, the lawyer himself is afforded the opportunity to play the bad boy, every little boy's fantasy involving power, boasting and dreaming wicked, but without the requirement of having to take responsibility. The public bows to this circumstance in recognition of the holy task that has been consummated, when a guilty party has prevailed via his lawyer and the proper legal rules. Indeed, a strong argument must be made that this should be so, in order to achieve the wider aims of a consistent justice system. There can certainly be justified passion in defending guilt in order to sustain valid legal rules, but then why is pride and passion so often absent in defending innocence? Why is the courage to push back against the legal system and unjust plea bargains absent in so many cases? The challenge to lawyers has become stopping the claim of innocence rather than defending it.

Lawyer disrespect for innocence may be considered a form of macho swagger. In Herman Melville's *Moby Dick*, the rational Starbuck offers men on their endangered whaling ship a choice: relieve a deranged Captain Ahab of his command and return safely to home, or continue onward in folly to certain doom in search of the killer whale. Seaman Stubb vehemently rejects the former proposition and replies to Starbuck, "The men would rather be kicked by Ahab than be knighted by the Queen of England." Like so much else that is wrong in the legal system, the seduction of the plea bargain has succeeded on the appeal of baser instincts, overwhelming Legal System 1, which is merely rational.

At a level we might call primitive, the level that often holds sway among men, innocence lacks a vital ingredient that demands respect. It has too much in common with weakness, with the child's world, with dependence on others. Legal innocence depends greatly on others, especially on a lawyer. For some adults– and surely as is experienced by many a child– good sport can be had by testing whether innocence can survive adversity placed in front of it intentionally and then to note, like a voyeur, how it does so when it does so.

MARK INGLIN

Bad lawyers use psychological coercion on innocent clients to avoid their own fears and professional responsibilities when confronting innocence. They will find a sustained claim of innocence by a client a personal affront and a challenge. If you work in a bordello, virginity is hardly what you value, but you may work hard for its extinction. Individuals habituated to lower levels of conduct and with poor standards often show disdain for others who exhibit higher principles. Maintaining true innocence is a higher principle. In 'hard-ass' legal surroundings, acting ethically to achieve higher standards does not win points.

Lawyers themselves have often been forced to compromise their values to earn a living and to accommodate a legal system that favors protecting itself. Why shouldn't the client also bend for the sake of practicality and for the smooth functioning of the system? 'Does the client think he's better than I am?' the lawyer may ask himself.

If justice were truly the goal of the legal system, as legal theory holds, then demonstrating innocence would be a score and a win for both teams. But when "winning" – as in career reward and status quo bias– takes priority, then innocence can be dismissed as too inconvenient and costly. Because he retains 'lawyer objectivity,' the lawyer has learned that innocence in his clients is something dispensable that must be put aside in the real world– like a child musician's dream of playing at Carnegie Hall.

In the intentional defeat of innocence by a betraying lawyer, would it be too extreme to compare that lawyer to a child molester? Or to the father who rationalizes that touching his own daughter inappropriately is teaching her about the real world? Innocence becomes a red flag of invitation to its elimination. Transgressions that revel in destroying innocence also share in common the state of denial. Awareness has departed and mere spinal cord reflexes have taken over, like the tongue of a frog slurping a fly. The innocent client today is treated to the ninety-five percent plea bargain statistic as his ordained destiny.

For the lawyer as well as police, a confession or an admission of guilt is a highly valued commodity that pushes aside the time-consuming, challenging consideration of innocence. A confession can render a defendant a criminal regardless of whether he actually committed the crime, while it also solves the crime. The legal system breathes a proverbial sigh of relief and closes a case successfully with a confession. On its face, this is entirely illogical: Shouldn't facts speak louder than other considerations? Shouldn't there be an intense drive for truth as to who committed a crime? This would certainly be true in a fact-based system. The legal system, however, through the application of Legal System 2 and contrary to the prevailing myth of objectivity, is primarily emotion based.

'What? You proved that you were not at the scene of the crime when it occurred? Then why did you confess? Surely you must have done something wrong.' The ubiquitous assumption is that those who are truly innocent would never confess to a crime that they did not commit, yet it happens all the time.

The *PBS Frontline* documentary "The Confessions" presents multiple, heartbreaking stories of false confessions and their practical finality in spite of later evidence to the contrary. In each case the accused succumbed to the pressure to confess. The 'crime' committed by the false confessor is really one that offends our Darwinian instincts. The confessor was too 'weak' to defend himself to the charge. While Legal System 1 contains provisions to reverse false confessions, Legal System 2 welcomes them, then deliberately impedes the process to reverse them, and often permanently.

False confessions are rampant in all cultures. In the USA the National Registry of Exonerations Statistics reports a rate of false confessions of 38 percent for people under 18-years-of-age, with rates estimated by other sources as roughly equal in adults or even as high as 70 percent for adults in Japan. We find it hard to believe that people will confess to crimes that they did not commit because it is unimaginable that we, ourselves, would confess to a crime that we did not commit. That may be true under ordinary circumstances and in a psychologically safe environment. Defending one's innocence in a criminal case is not an ordinary circumstance, nor does it take place in a safe environment. The stressors of police interrogation and lawyer coercion, with threats of dire penalties and fear of the unknown, can easily cause any defendant to capitulate to pressure and admit to crimes not committed.

When individuals are questioned about why they confessed to something they did not do, they invariably answer that they could not stand the imposed psychological tension any longer. Is this an outrageous statement? Some people can hold their hands above a candle flame longer than others. We logically conclude from that ... that some people can withstand more heat than others and we leave it there. No character judgments are made. But this is not so with confessions. Police and lawyers draw a great deal of significance from confessions, even if they are known to be false. The conclusion is that a confessor is inferior. Catch someone at a weak moment and it would seem that you have caught them forever.

Not illogically, false confessors reason that exculpatory evidence that can be presented later will show them to be incontestably innocent with the assistance, of course, of a lawyer. Rarely is this a good strategy. It turns out that you are excused to remove your hand from a hot flame because we all know hot flames can cause pain. Not enough of us know that psychological pressures by lawyers and police can also cause intolerable pain. We afford ourselves the pleasure of knowing that we would never do that and that we are therefore stronger.

THE COURAGE TO DEFEND

Prosecutors and lawyers will often use an analogy to war and combat for their experiences in a courtroom. The client, in that case, is the civilian, the defense lawyer his soldier. In this regard it is interesting to note that, during World War II, the

U.S. Military devised a surprisingly simple test to determine whether a man could face combat with courage. For example, men who panicked in amphibious landing craft as their boat approached an enemy beach under gunfire had to be weeded out. So military psychologists devised some simple questions to screen men, to determine who could not face deadly adversity: 'Have you ever stolen anything from work? Did you ever cheat on a test? Have you two-timed a girlfriend or wife?' It turns out that the answers to such questions can be used successfully to predict courage under fire. Men who led what might be called less than moral lives could often talk a good game before combat, but they tended to want to 'leave the boat' when they sensed danger.

As the military discovered, facing the possibility of danger or death references our memories back to the type of life that we have lived. At West Point, the cadet honor code reads, "I will not cheat, steal or tolerate those who do." The military has learned that it can teach courage by instilling high moral standards in its members. In turn, these standards lead to courage under fire. The reward for living by the code of "do the right thing even it's it the hard thing" pays off.

Considering the dysfunctional state of the legal system—an environment of deception, winning at all costs, and stubborn, macho denial of mistakes— the argument can be made that the legal system presents strong disincentives to the display of moral character and courage. In a legal system in which Legal System 2 is allowed to prevail, the environment actively encourages what we can call "anti-courage." Bad habits are instilled through their repeated success. Integrity, ethics and knowledge of Legal System 1 are counterproductive. No one goes to a bordello to find a virgin and, troublingly, we cannot look toward our legal system for a readily available supply of men of courage; they have either left the profession already, or they have been changed for the worse by the toxic legal environment.

What, exactly, does it take to defend another human being's claim of innocence? A defender of innocence must necessarily have retained a sense of respect for the innocence that is to be protected. Defending innocence requires empathy for the accused person. The lawyer must understand the value of the client's innocence and his right thereto. A lawyer with integrity, self-respect and courage will feel intense anxiety over the responsibility of protecting his client's innocence, but he will have the character to withstand that anxiety. He also accepts the responsibility as part of his professional obligation, just like a surgeon faces anxiety over the possible failure of an operation. The good lawyer does not 'leave the boat' under stress.

If a lawyer has failed in the past to carry out his professional responsibilities to vigorously defend an innocent client and the legal system, through its powers, has protected him from being held accountable, then the answer to the simple question "Did you ever betray a client" will loom large subconsciously in his future. As Wen Ho, a character in the book *The Manchurian Candidate,* aptly explained, "A man's first loyalty is to his conditioned nervous system." Lawyer habit will be to defeat his own client, the easy way to escape the anxiety of defending innocence with each subsequent client. To be sure, the lawyer may well intend to 'do it right' the next time, with the next innocent client. But somehow the client will always come to disappoint him.

The bad lawyer has relinquished ideals in order to gain practical, momentary rewards. He may not want his innocent client to be labeled a criminal, any more than the producer of defective auto parts wants an auto accident. But he rationalizes: 'Aren't we all guilty of some sin anyway, even if just original?'

Graduating from law school does not guarantee that someone will have the courage to stand before a jury and be a good trial lawyer. A lawyer must not only compile evidence and prepare testimony, he must also have the personal skills to convince a jury and, most importantly, be willing to face a loss. The opposing lawyer may be smarter or more aggressive. The judge may be unfavorably disposed due to history with the lawyer. Protecting the status quo in the legal community may also be a source of pressure. Not least, defending innocence and encountering the deeply personal emotions of another human being under such circumstances are among the most trying of all human experiences.

In Wisconsin, two lawyers who were not involved directly in a case wrote separate letters of personal support for a man who disclosed unethical conduct by a local lawyer in an essay that became public. Both letters lent support to a contention that there were serious problems with the lawyer and the legal community. The offended lawyer hired an 'enforcer' lawyer, a legal hit-man, who hauled one letter-writing lawyer before a judge, threatening damage to his career for expressing his critical view. Chastened, the lawyer disavowed his criticism. The other lawyer was fired outright by her law firm. There are heroes in battle, but no lawyer gets a medal for standing up to the bullies in his profession. In fact, he will face wrath from colleagues and even be forced to leave the profession.

For a lawyer to feel unconstrained in defense of a client, that defense must be viewed as neutral or without negative ramifications to the local power structure, colleagues in the system, law enforcement, or the lawyer himself. Except in an ideal world, pressures from these sources inhibit a lawyer and reduce his willingness to provide vigorous client defense. Legal system players quickly learn that the safe route in law is to use heavy-handed tactics to force settlements on weaker clients and enjoy repeated success thereby. To act otherwise requires courage, a virtue that is degraded and extinguished by the legal system environment.

PHISHERMEN AND PHOOLS

Two Nobel Prize winners in economics, George Akerlof and Robert Shiller, coined the term "phishing" to refer to a kind of angling that "phishermen"– banks, pharmaceuticals companies, and real estate agents, among others– do to hook "phools"– investors, car buyers, or homeowners etc.– into doing something that is in the interest of the phishermen.

To the list of phishermen we should add lawyers. and to the list of "phools" their clients.

Akerlof and Shiller explain that there are two kinds of phools: informational and emotional. Informational phools are victims of claims that are intentionally inaccurate and designed to mislead. Emotional phools are put off-course by either their own emotions or by cognitive biases. Among the emotions and biases, one of the most powerful is the client's need to think of his lawyer as trustworthy.

In a lawyer's office, a client will naturally respond favorably to promises to defend his claim of innocence– a human need that can be as important as life itself. Once hooked by the promise of defense, the client becomes an emotional phool, due to his need for legal representation and the hope of prevailing. That 'hook' can be remarkably difficult to undo– a fact not lost on the lawyer.

The lawyer knows that if a client drops a claim of innocence, his work will be far easier. But at exactly what point during the course of legal representation should that claim of innocence be dropped? Over the course of, for example, two years of legal representation, the lawyer has put in substantial time to justify a large legal bill by merely preparing for (or claiming to have prepared for) a trial. If the client can be coaxed (or coerced) to agree to a last-minute settlement just before a trial date, the extra revenue derived from going to trial may not compensate for the pressures, the risks, and the work required for a trial. A lawyer can earn a good living risk-free by preparing for trials that never take place.

Among the forces in play that favor the lawyer is the fact that the average client is almost always the entity with the least power, information and influence on the legal process. The client has little or no control over the procedure of defending his own innocence. Lawyers certainly know that, close to trial, if the defense lawyer has not yet extracted a plea bargain, the prosecution will apply crushing pressures on a defendant. Based on the ninety-five percent statistic, few clients will go the distance in such a fight.

A Swiss lawyer summed up the generally known circumstances nicely in one sentence when he instructed a client, "You will have to let me known when you have had enough and you wish to end it." "Enough" in this context meant enough of an overwhelmingly stressful legal process. To be sure, the defense lawyer never receives a phone call from the prosecutor, wherein he hears the words, 'I've had enough; tell your client I wish to settle.' But the fight must be fought, or else there is no reward for the lawyer. Obviously, a lawyer does not wish for his client to give in 'too early.' The phisherman must be rewarded by his catch.

If a lawyer promises to defend a client all the way to a trial in order to hook the client, the lawyer can almost certainly break that promise without practical cost because, well, who will hold him accountable? Circumstances can and do change during the course of legal representation, the lawyer will effectively argue. Because of the complexity of the process of legal defense and the human interactions that are involved, there are few practical limits to a lawyer if he has decided to use his powers in the system unethically. Standing up to the lawyer will be difficult for a client; proving wrongdoing by the lawyer will be even more difficult. Little will prevent the lawyer from insisting that he 'convinced' a client that his best option, regardless of innocence or guilt, was the plea bargain.

A lawyer works in a competitive marketplace; he is a businessman in a capitalist system. He needs work and remuneration and smooth operations in his work environment. Akerlof and Shiller, both of whom have studied human behavior extensively, reasonably explain that human weaknesses in a free market are exploited not due to intrinsic maliciousness or venality, but because market forces compel behavior by which phools are exploited.

Though it is tempting to do so– and this book admittedly does little to impede the notion, it would be misleading to label bad lawyers as evil. Not only misleading, but counterproductive, Far more useful is to consider the negative influence on the lawyer of the environment of the toxic legal system, which selects and molds its inhabitants for survival there.

In order to survive in the environment of Legal System 2 lawyers must have relinquished their moral values in favor of values related to career. A lawyer quickly learns that, in his chosen environment of criminal law, he can make a very good living merely preparing for trials that he never intends to be a part of. He also learns that applying Legal System 1 requires unnecessary self-sacrifice. As stated earlier, he has his rational excuse: there are not enough courtrooms to accommodate unfiltered need, not enough judges, not enough time to accommodate everyone who correctly assumes they have a constitutional right to a trial. And lawyers who do not exploit others will lose out to those lawyers who do.

A lawyer in Wisconsin called his client two weeks before trial in a case that had lasted sixteen months. "Everything has changed," he said, "We need to bargain this thing out."

"Why?" the client asked.

"New witnesses, and it isn't good. They see things differently from the way you claim," the lawyer argued, "The prosecution will have a field day now."

"Who are these witnesses?" the client asked.

"I cannot reveal that information at this time."

"What are they claiming that caused you to change your mind?"

"That what you contend isn't true, and they are credible people. They will make a good impression in court," the lawyer responded.

It turned out that there were no witnesses and no detrimental claims. The lawyer repeated a charade that he had performed successfully numerous times, falsely creating a turning point in the case to raise the client's anxiety and to induce the will to plea bargain.

We want to believe that a lawyer whom we have hired will be our gladiator, fighting the enemy– the false accuser– on our behalf. We do not wish to acknowledge that he is a human being in a pressure-filled environment subject to the same anxiety, self-doubt and fear as anyone else. It is a grave mistake, however, for a client to view his lawyer as above ordinary human emotions, especially those related to fear and loss. Yet typically when accused of a crime, clients are not emotionally strong enough to question their own lawyer, to employ game theory, or to evaluate local legal politics. The result is that the lawyer is relatively free to maneuver a client to avoid his own fears, at the expense of the client having his fears come true.

PHASES OF LAWYER REPRESENTATION

Like any animal, human beings act in conformity with the demands of their surroundings: public behavior versus private; cameras present versus none; access to power versus the opposite. The average legal client is fearful, relatively powerless and emotionally needy compared to his lawyer, who appears confident, powerful, and in control of the legal environment. It is the commonality of these influences on lawyer and client that leads to repeating patterns of behavior. These patterns are evident and can be described as phases of lawyer representation.

PHASE 1: SALE OF LAWYER SERVICES

The lawyer-client relationship starts with a sales pitch to the potential client to gain a signed contract for the lawyer to represent the client. An upfront fee known as a retainer is paid for future services. To hook his phish, the lawyer must choose his words carefully at the start of the interaction. Legal System 1 will often play a very important role here, as the lawyer explains how the law favors the innocent client. Positive aspects of a case are paraded in full view of a client while negative aspects are ignored. The lawyer makes clear that he 'likes' and 'respects' his potential client and he describes the potential client's demand for justice as 'a noble intent to be assisted.'

The lawyer makes it appear as if the legal battle that lies ahead will be 'us against them.' His assurance that 'we can go to trial, and we can prevail' will be spoken with seeming sincerity, even while he is well aware that there is a ninety-five percent chance that they will not go to trial. The two opposing concepts may do battle in the lawyer's mind, but there is only a five percent chance of one side winning. Client betrayal, when it comes, will require the form of, 'The client wisely changed his mind about going to trial.'

PHASE 2: UNDERMINING CLIENT INTENT WITH PSYCHOLOGICAL TOOLS

If marriage is the deathbed of romance, then paying the retainer is the end of legal fantasy. Payment means commitment by the client to the lawyer, but it starts strategic withdrawal by the lawyer. Payment and the contract herald a fundamental shift in power between the lawyer and the client. The client is now invested in his lawyer both financially and emotionally. The so-called sunk-cost effect, a term often used in economics to refer to a cost already incurred and unrecoverable, takes firm hold of a client, as do hope and trust.

To manipulate a client effectively after a contract has been signed, a lawyer needs to 1) reduce a client's desire to prove innocence, 2) disabuse the client's initial perception– actively promulgated by the lawyer– that the lawyer has the power to achieve the desired goal. These two retractions from the initial display of intent by the lawyer then provide 3) the power of the lawyer to betray the client by undermining previously held beliefs and expectations, thereby finally inducing a sense of helplessness, hopelessness and compliance. The client will now become fully susceptible to the *Lawyer Betrayal Syndrome.*

From the beginning of the professional relationship, a lawyer tries to gain the upper hand with a client by, as merely one example, disrespecting the client– a ploy taken from more than a few police playbooks on how to treat male criminal suspects. There are numerous ways for a lawyer to do this. The lawyer can, for example, make it clear that his time is more valuable than the client's. One criminal defense lawyer in Wisconsin often used a small, brown paper lunch bag kept at his desk. When a client arrives for an appointment at reception, he grabs the bag and, walking past the client, asks in an unfriendly tone, "Why are you here?" The client explains that an appointment had been set. The lawyer responds with, "Well, I missed my lunch (or breakfast). Now I'm going to eat something first. You will just have to wait."

The lawyer turns away and disappears. For someone new to the game and accused of committing a crime, such a show of disrespect immediately reinforces a feeling of inferiority and further dependence, putting the lawyer in greater control and beginning the process of manipulation toward a plea bargain.

As work begins on the client's defense, personal history and past conduct are called into question to induce a sense of guilt and insecurity. The client may have done wrong in various aspects of his life, but not related to the immediate accusation. He may have cheated on taxes, but he didn't kill Mrs. Jones. The fact is that there are clients who are innocent of a particular crime, yet they do not feel innocent with regard to the life that they have lived.

A lawyer who intends to have his client submit to a plea bargain arouses the client's sense of guilt for past behavior as part of a psychological grooming process. The client may be encouraged to unburden past transgressions couched in terms of revealing 'trouble-spots' in his background or character issues in order to, the lawyer claims, prepare for adequate legal defense. Financial, business, or sexual matters and drug use, unrelated to the case, can be used to remind the client later that, 'You are not perfect and the prosecutor will likely use the information against you at a trial.'

Questioning client history constitutes what lawyers defend as 'testing client resolve.' Just how determined is the client to go to trial? 'I don't want a client who can't stand up to the rigors of a trial,' the lawyer will claim. Will the client continue to tell the same story as time goes on? Do the facts continue to align? Remarkably, defense lawyers ubiquitously pride themselves on this tactic, boasting that 'The client must get past me, first, before he sees a courtroom.' The lawyer asks himself, 'Does this client have what it takes to go to trial?' Then he concludes, 'If not, that won't be my fault.'

Testing of a client by the lawyer comes to exhibit a classic Catch-22-type situation. If a client continues to insist on going to trial, the lawyer interprets this to mean that he has not applied adequate pressure to test the client. 'He still wants to go to trial? Passing my test doesn't mean that the client is ready for trial; it just means the testing has been too easy.' For lawyers who are plea bargain specialists, the level of confidence that their own expectations will be fulfilled precludes any other outcome. The big difference between the client and the lawyer here is that the lawyer has the power to see that his expectations are met; the client does not. The lawyer will disbelieve the innocent client before his very eyes and will continue to force through, at ever-higher emotional cost to the client, the plea bargain agenda.

Because the lawyer knows that it is highly unlikely that a case will proceed to trial, he also convinces himself that genuine preparation for trial is a waste of time. He is not getting dressed for a party that will never take place. The lawyer has psychological tools available to persuade a client; while the client has only the option of continuing with defense or not.

Not having prepared for trial, however, will leave the lawyer with no choice but to change a client's mind, perhaps at the last minute and in mounting desperation. The lawyer and client enter into a downward spiral of coercion that ensures client defeat. As trial approaches, the lawyer will do all that is necessary to coerce the client into a plea bargain.

In a case in Wisconsin a prominent lawyer known among his colleagues as 'the plea bargain master' was so desperate for a plea bargain close to a trial date that he used the plight of an abused child as a bargaining chip. Feeling unrestrained by ethical or legal limits, he informed his client that his child might suffer further abuse from the other parent if he continued to hold out for a trial rather than plea bargain. When the client asked for intervention by child protective services, the lawyer refused to provide the necessary verification, insisting that there had to be a plea bargain before he released any information. No action to protect the child could be taken without the lawyer's consent; the client was essentially mute compared to the lawyer's perceived credibility and his influence.

In Switzerland, a defense lawyer who billed his client for two years of trial preparation simply withdrew from the case just prior to the trial because the client refused to settle. It later emerged that the lawyer had not submitted exculpatory evidence to the court by the required deadline, which meant certain defeat at trial. The lawyer had bet on a settlement, but lost. However, the lawyer then relied on his relationship with the judge to avoid professional responsibility for dropping the client at the last minute. The judge simply refused to hold the lawyer accountable. The lawyer's strategy paid off. He had earned money claiming to have prepared for trial, but avoided the emotional burden of trial, forcing that onto the client.

In Wisconsin, a defense lawyer failed to submit an extensive defense witness list that had been prepared for trial. The lawyer was so convinced of a last-minute plea bargain in the courtroom on the day of trial that he also failed to bring along vital evidence for the defense. The judge demanded the trial go forward. The gross negligence was later concealed by the appellate lawyer and, in part, also by the judge. For the appeal, the client had received promises of exposure of earlier lawyer negligence, but the appeal failed to mention any misconduct. The intentional oversight and failure to present evidence of earlier lawyer misconduct in the appeal, in turn, ensured that the misconduct could not be broached again, as such was prohibited by Legal System 1.

The simple fact that goes widely unrecognized, and the essence of the power imbalance between and lawyer and a client, is that the lawyer is permitted to apply endless pressure on the client, but if the client puts pressure on the lawyer to do his job, the lawyer can take his ball and go home!

The psychological tactic of applying emotional stress in order to break down client resistance is highly effective and the bad lawyer's best friend. Applying stress rather than using a fact-finding approach has been shown to lead to false confessions in a police interrogation setting; the same approach can lead to plea bargaining. Research shows that applying emotional stress leads to a suggestible nervous system, regardless of guilt or innocence. The human brain reacts to stress that exceeds its capacity by yielding to the dominant force, accepting suggestions for behavior, for example by a lawyer promoting a plea bargain.

When asked, individuals who have confessed to crimes that they did not commit have repeatedly stated that they confessed in order to relieve the extreme emotional tension of the interrogation. The same can be true for coerced plea bargains. With the police, however, a suspect at least knows that stress will probably be short-lived; he is often expecting the stress, and he usually does not consider the police to be trustworthy. The lawyer, on the other hand, has ample time to apply emotional pressure, the client is not expecting betrayal and, unfortunately, the lawyer is usually trusted.

In the case of a police interrogation, eliminating the stress of the procedure, the stress of the moment, is the priority. The rationalization that a false confessor puts forth is that, because he knows that he is innocent of the crime, his innocence can be proven later by a lawyer. Such an option essentially disappears completely after a plea bargain.

PHASE 3: CLIENT ROLLOVER

In phase 3 of lawyer representation, the lawyer has had the opportunity for extensive billing, the client is emotionally and financially invested, not infrequently emotionally drained, and ripe for rollover. Rollover refers to a change in client thinking as a result of psychological coercion. It takes advantage of the heightened mental suggestibility as the client's resistance has diminished. If an old way of thinking causes too much stress and pain, a new view of the world is in order. A temporary fusion of beliefs with those of the lawyer, i.e. the plea bargain, is the ready option to avoid further stress. Psychologically, it is the equivalent of being allowed to remove a hand from atop a candle flame.

William James, in his book *The Varieties of Religious Experience: A Study of Human Nature*, exquisitely describes how the same destabilizing mental tension that can arise in a lawyer's office occurs in religious conversion experiences, tipping a mind into another belief. James describes the unease and agitation that an individual feels before he comes to settle into a new view of the world: unease, anxiety, spiritual discomfort, a sense that all is not well. Old habits and thoughts are finally thrown aside entirely, providing peace of mind to the converted, at least temporarily.

A lawyer rolls a client over because clients are easier to deceive and manipulate than fellow lawyers, prosecutors and seasoned members of the legal system. While those individuals have bought into and understand the game of threats and fears that play out in the legal system, clients/defendants, with their lack of experience, can be counted on to respond as repeat patterns of behavior have demonstrated. The lawyer can employ tactics that could not be applied ethically or legally in most other circumstances, because a lawyer or possibly law enforcement could stop such tactics. In the privacy of the lawyer's office no such limits to psychological coercion can be enforced.

Some lawyers crassly use financial threats to induce client capitulation to a plea bargain. Despite earlier agreements, a lawyer can flat-out refuse to proceed to a trial unless the client pays more money. Earlier guarantees are meaningless. The lawyer will claim that he needs to invest more effort than anticipated— more detective work, more paralegal work and so on. There is no practical way to prevent such threats. In one instance in Wisconsin, a lawyer demanded an extra seven thousand dollars for weekend preparation two days before a trial. The client paid; the lawyer spent several hours going over old material, all of which turned out to be merely a final effort to insist on a plea bargain.

In practice, no one can or will hold the lawyer to his earlier promises regarding fees, or anything else. No judge can force a lawyer to do a good job for his client. If the client doesn't pay, the lawyer will not act or he will drag his feet. If the client does pay, as in this case, the lawyer can still drag his feet.

A lawyer can retain a depraved, paradoxical sense of self-worth and pride if, instead of using financial coercion, he demonstrates to the client that he is emotionally unfit to go onward to a trial and must therefore plea bargain. Ominously, the defeat of a client may also satisfy a less obvious and little discussed emotional need on the part of the bad defense lawyer.

Success in various competitions among human beings is associated with feelings of potency, superiority and wellbeing, and is also tied in with sexual conquest. The schoolyard bully enjoys lowered blood pressure after he trounces a victim. Testosterone levels jump for a dominant individual after physical dominance has been established over another person. Psychological dominance can have the same effect. These good feelings, like any others, draw certain individuals to engage in conduct that provides them, momentarily. Momentary dominance can be achieved by the act of betrayal. The effect of a betrayal is the 'betrayer's high,' the release of the drug of choice from the brain's medicine chest. Disturbingly, as with our brown lunch-bag criminal defense lawyer above, achieving dominance through emotional abuse can turn out to be a highly successful legal strategy, aside from providing an emotional kick. The client, of course, is at the opposite end of the strategy and will show a reduction in testosterone levels and dopamine, due to the awareness of his own defeat and subjugation.

There is a scene in the film *American Psycho* in which the protagonist, a successful but psychologically twisted businessman, runs into a homeless person in a dark, deserted alley. The businessman stabs the homeless person repeatedly in the chest and kills him, but not before first quietly and deliberately talking to him, holding out the prospect of money, raising his hopes that he might receive aid. The disparity in status– wealth and success versus poverty and failure– disgusted the businessman and stoked his deep depravity. Not only would the killing have been devoid of its meaning without the algorithmic prelude of raised expectations, it might even have been impossible. Most men aren't chain-saw killers; they only act that way in the business world. A lawyer's business is defending the innocent, a task that leads certain men only to find their inner depravity.

The bad lawyer has manifold ways of increasing a client's anxiety about his legal circumstances. He is at liberty to tell dispiriting untruths, orchestrate repeat delays, and schedule false venues. After all, who will stop him, even if deceit can be proven?

Rare is the client who has the confidence, while innocent and under a legal accusation, to thoroughly question or push back on a lawyer's strategy. He is forced to wonder whether what the lawyer tells him is true. He is dependent on his lawyer's view of the case. The client is told one thing while the legal strategy may be headed in a completely different direction, the direction of ensuring the plea bargain.

The pretense of working together with a client to achieve justice diminishes as the lawyer comes closer to a trial date and focuses on his own need for the plea bargain. He has engaged his strategy to ensure billable hours for services, while at the same time softening the will of the client to resist.

LAWYER TOOLS FOR BETRAYAL

A lawyer has at his disposal an arsenal of tricks, traps and stressors that can 'spare a client trial.' His office is a unique environment where power and vulnerability meet in an intimate space. The lawyer can effectively do as he pleases in the privacy (confidentiality) of his office and feel assured that there will be no meaningful oversight, nor will there be practical accountability. Subsumed under the guise of 'testing the client,' the lawyer uses tactics to emotionally undermine the client to the point at which he submits to a plea bargain.

As anxiety, exhaustion, and fears accumulate for the client, the emotional cost of maintaining a claim of innocence can become unsustainable. Even if the client viewed his innocence as something important to be defended at any cost at the beginning of his legal representation, over time this desire diminishes due to the same pressures experienced by a suspect who can no longer withstand police interrogation; the need to ease mental and emotional anxiety becomes as urgent as the need to ease physical pain.

The tools that a lawyer applies to increase psychological pressure and finally to betray the client include the following:

1. **Exploitation of expectations:** Raising and dashing client expectations, whether related to the law in the form of Legal System 1 or in any other of numerous ways, is one very important element of lawyer betrayal. The excuse that 'things have changed' represents the cheap lubricant that greases the retraction from any lawyer promise made.
2. **Time, deadlines.** The lawyer controls time and is at liberty to manipulate it. Things happen when the

lawyer wants them to happen, regardless of how anxious that makes the client. The lawyer makes last minute demands on the client under pressure, claiming for example that missing a suddenly imposing deadline will diminish or eliminate the client's chances at prevailing. If the client questions these practices, the lawyer will deny them or warn that the client is interfering with 'lawyer strategy.' The responsibility for a bad outcome will rest with the client.
3. **Venues.** The lawyer can raise or lower client anxiety by scheduling various venues and appointments, some of which may be greatly desired by the client, others unpleasant and emotionally threatening. If a meeting is anticipated by the client, it will be cancelled close to the expected date. The pattern of repeatedly making and then breaking promises, starting with minor issues such as missed appointments, can exhaust a client emotionally, weakening the will to continue defense.
4. **Providing false information.** The lawyer is at liberty to provide false information regarding potential witnesses, the prosecution, the attitude of the judge, results of the lawyer's own investigation of the client, and so on. He may do all of this while assuring the client that he is collecting evidence for his defense when, in fact, the evidence or the purported evidence may serve only to bolster the argument for a plea bargain.

5. **Poor communications.** One of the many complaints registered against lawyers with professional oversight boards is "failure to communicate." The lawyer deliberately fails to return phone calls or respond to emails.
6. **Blaming the client.** The lawyer will find ways to make the client feel responsible for his own current, adverse situation, putting and keeping the client on the defensive, making him feel dependent and inferior.
7. **Rejection.** The lawyer who bonded with and 'liked' the client at the start of the legal representation changes his attitude toward the client to one of disrespect or even aggressive dislike, once the intent becomes rollover. The lawyer turns intolerant, dismissive, and rude. This is sometimes initiated immediately after the retainer has been paid.
8. **Threats of abandonment.** As the professional relationship progresses, the client comes to need the lawyer emotionally far more than the lawyer needs the client. The lawyer will drop reminders of how difficult the case will become if the client needs to acquire a new lawyer.
9. **Deliberately provoking anger.** Repeatedly provoking anger in a client can lead to his emotional exhaustion, making it easier for the lawyer to dominate the client and change his mind.
10. **Intentional inefficiency.** There is no penalty for a lawyer who deliberately works inefficiently. Each

legal case is unique; there are no set standards that are meaningful.
11. **Racial intimidation.** In some cases lawyers will frighten their clients into a plea bargain by convincing clients of color that they will face an all-white jury inclined to be prejudiced against their claim of innocence.

Reported by The Marshall Project– in Idaho v. White– a black man named Robert Wayne White tried to retract a guilty plea in a case of sexual assault on a white woman. The defendant contended that he had been inappropriately counseled by his lawyer that he "would not be able to win a jury trial" in a majority white county in an overwhelmingly white state. The argument was rejected by the state's judges. Counsel, the Idaho judges determined, "was strategically sound because it was based on his practical experience."

In "When the Threat of a White Jury is an Interrogation Tool," an article written by legal analyst Andrew Cohen states that, "Judges seem to be far more forgiving of defense attorneys who essentially counsel clients of color to take a guilty plea because they won't stand a chance in a 'white' justice system." The threat of an unfair jury is an effective way to quickly replace any "misguided" desire for claiming innocence and seeking justice. Racial intimidation is a long-standing tool used by lawyers to betray their clients.

A combination of many of the above, listed tools was used by a defense lawyer in the notorious case of Laurie

'Bambi' Bembenek, who was falsely accused of murder in Milwaukee. Bembenek, a former Milwaukee police officer, garnered nationwide attention and was portrayed in the made for television movie *Woman on the Run: The Lawrencia Bembenek Story*. What the public did not discover was that, in an attempt to keep legal system wrongdoing concealed, her lawyer devastated Bembenek emotionally by shuttling her repeatedly from jailhouse to courthouse for venues with no purpose other than to cause emotional and physical fatigue and to raise expectations that were dashed repeatedly. That same lawyer also imposed control over his clients at the stage of their expected release on bail using the tactic of raising and dashing expectations.

In another case in Wisconsin, a criminal defense lawyer used psychological manipulation to undermine his client for a coerced admission of guilt despite a strong, continued sense of his own innocence. The case involved a young ex-Marine who ran over a woman's foot on his way home from a party. She had clung to his pick-up truck while he drove away. He was unaware of the accident until the police arrested him the next morning for hit and run driving. The defense lawyer promised he could prove the Marine's claim of innocence in court. There were favorable witnesses; a jury would understand the circumstances.

The former Marine never went to trial. Instead, the lawyer used false claims of having come upon detrimental evidence and opposing witnesses, broke promises that raised expectations for meetings requested by his client, and provoked guilt for unrelated conduct earlier in the Marine's life. After one year of psychological manipulation the Marine was emotionally exhausted and confused. He pleaded guilty and accepted a plea bargain.

"It wasn't my lawyer's fault, really, I guess," the Marine ironically explained afterwards, angry at himself, "He was tougher than I was, as I see it today. I should have kept claiming my innocence. I didn't run over anybody intentionally." In fact, in the end the Marine broke down emotionally in that lawyer's office, defeated in the sense that the lawyer had aimed for, with the lawyer literally and symbolically towering over him.

For the bad lawyer, such an emotional breakdown is as good as guilt; the two are synonymous. When it was suggested later that the Marine register a complaint against his lawyer (who had gained a reputation for client betrayal), he explained that he no longer had the energy to do so; he just wanted to forget that the incident had happened. This case is typical and highly representative. The lawyer had successfully switched the agenda from the two of them, lawyer and client, battling the system to attain justice, to the lawyer battling his client by psychological means. The Marine had also confused his physical 'toughness' with emotional durability, blaming himself rather than pointing out unethical conduct, just as many lawyers come to fully expect.

A lawyer knows that breaking a promise to go to a trial by a specific date– and many other promises– can cause client anger and lead to a weakening of client will. Also, paradoxically, if done properly, the client will eventually assume responsibility for his own failure to defend innocence, as in the above case. The client will be shown to have been too weak for the demands of the legal system— a sin on its own— thereby absolving the lawyer of responsibility. After all, the client must be seen as voluntarily agreeing to a plea bargain or a settlement. In gaining the betrayer's high, the lawyer must remain wary of coercion that is too overt; he is not a thug. Moreover, he will need to have a client's voluntary signature at some point. Lawyer betrayal is an art, not a trade.

While contrived complexity and unnecessary delays are generally unfavorable in the typical working world, the legal system rewards lawyers for inefficiency, making it another tool that benefits the lawyer. The longer a case takes, the more a lawyer can earn and the wearier a client becomes. Effective tactics to extend billing include conducting investigations entirely unnecessary to a case and taking far more time than necessary for simple procedures. On the other hand, beneficial investigations that may implicate members of the legal system in wrongdoing, even when the client demands them, can be delayed, modified or avoided entirely.

One lawyer in Milwaukee made extra money by deliberately forgetting to bring along files necessary in cases that required attendance at a deposition. The lawyer billed for the time required both for his secretary to deliver the files to the deposition, and for his time waiting for the files.

LAWYERS BROKEN BAD

Because it is difficult to prove that forgetting is intentional, or that a part of an investigation took less time than claimed etc., a client will rarely contest a bill. Lawyers, of course, know this. A client who wishes to contest a bill needs to provide reasoning. How many clients will challenge a lawyer's bill, and on what basis? The lawyer might take offense. We sense that it is best not to annoy an attending physician in hospital; clients feel the same way about annoying a lawyer. Moreover, the lawyer has the advantage of using the law at a discount to force payment of a bill.

In a case involving extradition, a New Zealand lawyer billed thousands of dollars for time spent on research. As luck would have it, the client became romantically involved with another lawyer who investigated the case and discovered that the claimed legal research had merely been photocopied from a similar case. Some of the pages of research still contained the original, incorrect case number. Looking up the original case and the photocopying may have taken a few hours, but the lawyer charged the client for ten times as much work. In a rare case of a hand caught in the cookie jar, the cheating lawyer was forced to return 75 percent of the billing.

The deliberate psychological destabilization of a legal client by psychological means to prevent the pursuit of innocence to the point of a trial is illegal, but it is also encouraged and nearly impossible to prove. Regulatory authorities are not eager to invite complaints from clients regarding ethics violations by their lawyer. They will respond by issuing a form letter with instructions to 'file a complaint,' then drag their feet. If the client does formally complain, a lawyer can often claim that the client was psychologically unstable as a result of 'the normal stresses of the ordeal.' The lawyer can enjoy success with this claim because the environment of legal accusation alone is often enough to cause poor psychological health; betrayal only contributes to the problem. Even if a client is aware and willing to disclose lawyer wrongdoing, where does he find the energy for an extensive fight with his own lawyer?

In the Canton of Zurich, Switzerland, individuals must pay a fee to register a complaint of violation of ethics or professional duty against their lawyer. Eight-hundred Swiss francs must be deposited before the responsible authorities claim that they will investigate. The deposit, it is explained, will be returned if the complaint is found to have "merit." No statistics are provided on how often such a return of funds occurs, while the term "merit" remains poorly defined. Such a burden on a client is apparently unique to Switzerland. Neither New Zealand, the USA, Canada nor the UK charge a fee for an ethics complaint by a client against his lawyer.

Years ago I spoke to Laurie Bembenek, after her ordeal with lawyer betrayal. I asked her to contribute to my first book, *Beyond Outrage*, on the topic. She was sympathetic but justifiably pleaded mental exhaustion, even though it had been years since she was released from prison. She had to let her lawyer off the hook, she explained, because she no longer had the stamina to confront him or immerse herself in painful memories.

The perverse reality is that the more a lawyer beats up a client emotionally, the less likely the client is to cause the lawyer trouble. An equivalency might be drawn to the cop who shoots to kill when he has a choice, because a kill avoids any possible messy legal liability. Laurie died in 2010, beat-up thoroughly and with impunity by a dysfunctional, venal legal system in Milwaukee, and well-aided by her own lawyer.

CERTAIN LAWYER REWARDS

It is said that without courage there is no other virtue. It takes considerable courage to challenge the local legal status quo on behalf of an outsider– the client; it takes courage to avoid using readily available lawyer tools that make a lawyer's life far easier. As we have seen, the legal environment is the wrong place to look for courage. Instead, it teaches that the opposite of courage is not only safe for a lawyer, but also leads to career success. Lawyer concerns for the status quo and its impact on careers therefore pollute the entire legal system.

Success and rewards, monetary and otherwise, lead lawyers to rationalize/justify/employ client betrayal in lieu of courage. The considerations cannot be dismissed because they influence a lawyer every working day:

- The justice system is overloaded;
- Fear of possible adverse impact on members of the legal community;
- Annoying judges with demands for trials;

- Preparing for trials is hard work entailing risks; it isn't necessary;
- Client betrayal offers emotional rewards;
- Everyone else is doing it, and it works. So why not?

Lawyers generally are not revolutionaries or idealists. They are businesspeople, but repeat business is not a significant consideration for a criminal defense lawyer, given the esoteric nature of the work. The questions that a successful businessman-lawyer must ask himself when submitting evidence, making statements to the media concerning a client, or filing an appeal are: Is there any detriment to my career or my legal community if I defend this client vigorously? Who else must I also think about protecting, right along with my client?

The existence of a common legal work environment, with its hierarchical pressures, accounts for repeating patterns of lawyer behavior that we see and that have begun to arouse attention. As with the police, the dismissal of lawyer anecdotes, i.e. isolated lawyer horror stories, is shifting to a concern that the anecdotes reflect general truth. The general truth is that lawyers quickly discover that they benefit financially and professionally from utilizing manipulative tactics on clients. Done with skill, under the favorable conditions of unequal power, a lawyer needs never go to trial, can blame his clients for their failures to continue with their own defense, and enjoy a financially lucrative practice.

Lawyers feel compelled to maneuver clients toward plea bargains for reasons that go beyond the lack of legal system capacity, but that also fall short of outright attribution to psychopathology– although lawyers do rank high on scales that measure psychopathology. Strong, interpersonal bonds naturally form between individuals in the legal system as a result of shared history and intense emotional encounters. If wrongdoing can be concealed to prevent change and loss within the legal tribe, that path will be highly attractive to any individual in that tribe. If the choice is between doing harm to a fellow warrior or to an outsider client of less consequence, the client becomes expendable.

If a lawyer particularly clever at forcing plea bargains has never had a client 'get past me' to a trial, then he is also likely to see every client as having an emotional breaking point at which he will plea bargain rather than continue to a trial. Working to reach that breaking point is a temptation that becomes a challenge and finally an outright obsession. A bad lawyer in effect grooms his client for the eventual, emotionally-wrenching reversal of lawyer-fostered client expectations. The abrupt reversal of expectations leads to symptoms of confusion, emotional exhaustion and depression. These symptoms, in turn, make it less likely that a client will object to or report ethical violations by his lawyer. If a client who initially vowed to maintain his innocence is too exhausted or fearful to go to trial as a result of the legal defense process, the lawyer absolves himself of all responsibility because 'the client did not have the strength that legal defense demands.'

The bad lawyer who lacks the courage to practice law ethically cannot enjoy victory by the rules of Legal System

1; he can, however, enjoy a perverted feeling of victory by rationalizing, for example, that he spared the client ten years in prison in exchange for two years. The loss of the client's dignity, the violation of his express will and the disregard for innocence are not only discounted in the law business, they become symbols of what needs to be shed or rejected in order to be in line with the real, practical world. While an abused spouse or a coerced employee, for example, has the option of calling on powerful agencies for help– not least including a lawyer– the abused legal client is effectively on his own.

Challenging the status quo in a community on behalf of a legal system outsider– the client– is one of the most formidable challenges that a lawyer faces. The recent exposure of culpatory information against entertainer Bill Cosby illustrates the point. Year ago, a number of credible women came forth to accuse Cosby of rape and sexual harassment, only to be sent away by lawyers and by law enforcement. The issue was not one of lack of evidence, but rather a lack of willingness to challenge an entertainment icon and a powerful status quo. The evidence against Cosby today is probably no stronger than it was when the crimes were ostensibly committed. Instead, an environment now exists that is more favorable to believing the accusations and entertaining the evidence.

For lawyers, the ubiquity of creeping success using unethical methods that require no courage or challenge to the status quo leads to what engineering disciplines refer to as the "normalization of deviance." Little by little the ethical/legal rules are broken with no associated costs. The proper limits thus continue to be tested and stretched anew until, finally, the system undergoes major failure. The circumstances attract reform and effective limits are again imposed.

PART 3

CLIENT BURDEN

THE POWER OF ACCUSATION

IN HIS SUICIDE note, the Japanese film director Juzo Itami claimed that only by death at his own hands could he adequately demonstrate innocence to a false accusation that had been made against him. Being accused of a crime is a life-altering event for an accused individual. The act of accusing someone of a crime is an act of aggression.

Accusation provokes earliest memories and the fears associated with those memories. Anxieties and discomforts arise from referring back to the earliest sources of approval and love. Accusation immediately raises questions of love's permanence and the threat of abandonment. It is the fear of abandonment that hands a lawyer one of his most powerful weapons. For this and many other reasons, the environment of accusation is obviously dangerous to an accused individual.

While a suicide following an accusation may be rare, the feeling that something inside oneself has died is universal for an innocent individual after being falsely accused. Momentum towards an assumption of guilt builds rapidly against an accused individual, right from the start of an accusation. He or she is no longer on equal footing with the community, especially with their lawyer, as accusation works in a bad lawyer's favor. Even if an accused individual is proven innocent later, the damage has been done and his life will never be the same.

If the psychic tension triggered in an accused individual by a false accusation is enough to lead to suicide, then the accuser need prove nothing further about the validity of his accusation. The accuser in this case is the clear winner in the court of public opinion. Suicide is often viewed as an admission of guilt. It may, however, also indicate a depleted will to persist following a wrongful accusation. There is no way to know whether a suicide was the means to relieve the pressure of guilt or the pressure of accusation.

The highly successful trial lawyer, Gerry Spence, once remarked that, "Anyone who hasn't been in trouble isn't worth a damn." If Spence had been a psychologist or an economist, he might have said it another way: Anyone who hasn't experienced loss isn't worth a damn. To be accused of a crime is to be in trouble. To be in trouble can mean the loss of friends, even abandonment by loved ones, and the need for a lawyer. Spence's remark was made in reference to the fact that people who have not been in trouble or experienced significant loss themselves often fear the fact that someone else... someone they know is actually in 'trouble.'

Perhaps ironically, some aspect of innocence must necessarily have been lost by a potential defender of innocence in order to defend someone else's innocence vigorously. That loss of innocence, however, should have been earned the hard way, through having in the past experienced the importance of loyalty and developed the courage needed to face one's own imperfections or worldly trials, or through having fought against an unrighteous enemy or even a false accusation. Spence, in his law career, observed that the predilection to avoid seeing any evil in the world, or to turn away from uncomfortable circumstances involving law or authority figures, is a vestige of childhood, the un-ripened soul 'not worth a damn' in an adult.

Like many lawyers, Spence had seen the initial willingness of potential witnesses or defenders of innocence to come forth with information helpful to an accused individual, then watched as the intent evaporated as a trial date approached. Here again, reference can be made to the simple questions asked by the U.S. Military about the type of life an individual has lived, and its effect when the future presents threatening challenge.

The possible personal consequences of testifying in court to defend innocence can begin to register fully in the mind of an individual who intends to stand up for justice. A less than exemplary past can inhibit the courage to confront the threat of, for example, a prosecutor at a trial asking uncomfortable questions. But it isn't just the prosecutor who can pose threats to a potential defense witness. The defense lawyer who is intent on the plea bargain can raise red flags in the mind of a supporter, causing an erosion of support for the client and another reason to plea bargain.

There are lawyers who are drawn toward the feeling of power when they meet a desperate, accused and innocent client. Accusation leads to the need of the accused to be believed, protected and defended. Openly exhibiting the need for defense and the associated perception of relative weakness can, in the extreme, draw the sadist like a flower draws a bee. The good feelings that can arise from having power over an accused individual can lead to a mentality aimed entirely at keeping the accused person– the client– weak, and not at confronting the prosecution. Relationships based on need combined with the feeling of wanting to be needed are all around us, in society. There is no reason to assume that this same dynamic plays no role in the lawyer-client relationship.

The lawyer-client relationship, its intensity of emotions and its usually extended duration of interaction lead to another consideration: how will the professional relationship end? If a client prevails, he pays his bill, says "thank you" and "good-bye." But keeping a client needy includes the reward of not facing an ending and perhaps, in the mind of a lawyer, always being needed. One Swiss lawyer, who relied on the tools of client betrayal with his clients, rewarded this conjecture with a strange but, on reflection, not surprising remark. In reference to the television drama *True Detective* he complained that, "I don't watch the endings to any dramas. I shut them off beforehand; they make me uncomfortable." This lawyer, in his legal practice, also shut his clients off before the end, as he threatens to refuse to go to court if a client fails to settle under his coercive efforts.

MARK INGLIN

BUT YOU CAN ALWAYS LEAVE A BAD LAWYER!

Those who are inexperienced with the legal system may believe that a client can always leave a bad lawyer, just like leaving a bad doctor or dentist. However, leaving one lawyer for another is difficult; financial entanglements as well as emotional bonding take place in the extended lawyer-client relationship. There are sunk-costs to consider: A retainer has been paid. Will any money be returned? Will legal files be made available efficiently to a new lawyer? There are many documents to photocopy, reread and rehash. A new lawyer needs to be oriented, a more or less complex task depending on the legal history. The bad lawyer will also play on the client's separation anxieties and fears of abandonment. 'Will another lawyer even take this case, if I decide to drop you?' he hints as a threat to his client, 'You have given me so much trouble already, I can hardly recommend you to anyone else.'

In a Wisconsin case in which a client refused to settle and in which the lawyer reneged on an agreement to go to trial, the lawyer not only resigned from the case, but left the country for a vacation in Scotland with the client's files left in disarray. When the new lawyer asked the absent lawyer's firm for the files, it turned out that they had simply been dumped in a banker's box, with various, other legal responsibilities also neglected. The judge ignored a vehement complaint by the client.

When a Swiss client complained to a judge that he had difficulties finding a new lawyer following his lawyer's refusal to go to trial close to the trial date, the judge scoffed openly in court at the claim, as if such refusals were impossible. The client offered to provide the judge the names of lawyers who had refused the case on that basis. Retracting her bravado, she shook her head and explored the topic no more.

Contrary to myth and lawyer self-promotion, a client's relationship with a lawyer is highly emotional. Consider the circumstances of this relationship: close, private interactions between two individuals, the sharing of highly personal information, great need meeting power, the building of trust and expectations between two human beings. We have extreme inequality of social/media influence, extreme inequality of credibility, a high state of suggestibility for the client and the practical inability for his self-defense if he is abandoned by the lawyer. All of this creates an emotional relationship and a classic environment ripe for emotional abuse.

In fact, there are few relationships that reach the level of emotional intensity and involvement of the lawyer-client relationship when the defense of innocence is at stake. Lawyers are not psychotherapists; they are not trained for, nor do they aspire to provide emotional comfort. Yet the client finds himself turning to his lawyer for emotional reassurance. Even if a client is seeing a psychologist while being represented by a lawyer, the client senses that the source of power and salvation in his case resides with the lawyer. The lawyer can solve the problem of a false accusation, the psychologist cannot. The psychologist, however, can sympathize with the anxiety and psychological regression exhibited by the client/patient, while perhaps not directly wishing to address the issue of the client's own lawyer undermining the client in preparation for rollover. After all, the lawyer may have recommended the client to his favored psychologist. Will the psychologist explain to his patient that his lawyer may be causing his symptoms?

The one-way direction in neediness between a client and a lawyer is readily demonstrated by simply noting who initiates phone calls and emails, and how quickly they are answered. The traffic is usually one way. Phone calls are made to a lawyer's office, the lawyer delays in answering, not the reverse. The lawyer calls the client and the client anxiously returns the call without delay. In a case in Switzerland, a client who kept a detailed record of his communications with his lawyer rarely phoned the lawyer. On one occasion the lawyer phoned the client and, during what turned into a heated discussion, the lawyer accused the client of wasting his time with phone calls. "It was surreal," the client commented, "He was talking to me as if I had been some sort of generic client. He was unaware that I was not following the usual pattern to which he had become accustomed until I called his attention to that fact."

The lawyer's ability to mask his own emotional dependence in the relationship with his client is reinforced by the fulfillment of a pattern that the lawyer knows well and expects: client neediness turns into capitulation followed by a plea bargain *if* the lawyer turns against the client using his available tools. Without emotional bonding taking place between a client and his lawyer, it would be difficult to change the mind of a client who insists on innocence, and to have that client accept a plea settlement.

Changing a mind that holds firm to a meaningful belief requires emotional engagement. Fire and brimstone preachers know this phenomenon well. Religions that conjure emotions are far more successful at recruiting new members than are doctrines that appeal to the intellect. Being innocent of a crime and wishing to prove such can be among the most strongly held beliefs. The ninety-five percent statistic on plea bargaining could never withstand objective interactions between a lawyer and his client.

The dynamic of a relationship with unequal power is often played out in ordinary romantic relationships. Two people meet and then struggle for dominance, for a sense of personal security. If the needy partner becomes too demanding, the other partner instinctively pulls away. The bond between them, however, has not disappeared; it merely submerges in the consciousness of the less needy, *seemingly* more powerful partner. If the more needy person retreats emotionally, this allows the bond to be felt again by the overtly less needy partner.

The typical lawyer-client relationship makes tactical emotional retreat from the lawyer by the client virtually impossible. How much abuse will a client tolerate from a lawyer, if he thinks that lawyer can set him free? The client can be counted on to yield and remain dependent because the client has the least power, seeks his goal intensely, and cannot (or dares not) withdraw from the demands of the case. The lawyer thereby gains a sense of power and security by knowing how very difficult it is going to be for the client to retreat. Disrespect for the client emerges and is tolerated by the client. In turn, the lawyer loses respect for his client. If the client does attempt to retreat, the lawyer can inflict considerable harm in the form of his rejection and abandonment. The client is trapped in a one-sided emotional relationship. This is why a Swiss criminal defense lawyer refers to his own clients as "weakest links" in the process of administering his cases.

Leslie Abramson, a premier criminal defense lawyer, neatly addresses the paradoxes of lawyer perceptions, superficial claims of lawyer objectivity, and the true nature of the lawyer-client relationship in her book *The Defense is Ready*. Remarkably, Abramson boasts of her caring deeply for her clients and coming emotionally close to them, including having dinners with clients and their relatives. She engages in this seemingly paradoxical behavior in order to do her job effectively, to avoid ennui, self-recrimination and guilt later on.

Abramson's attitude is the opposite of the simplistic wisdom espoused by many lawyers, that emotional involvement leads to the opposite of objectivity. The fact that sensitive, proper concern for a client actually leads to effective legal defense is a paradox only if false reasoning is applied in understanding the nature of an emotional bond.

Lawyers too often operate under the false assumption that reasoning at the conscious or intellectual level alone is enough to practice law. The term for this concept, misused, is 'retaining objectivity.' Lawyers, being unschooled in emotional health, are therefore misled about what constitutes appropriate emotional involvement in a case. The conscious denial of incoming emotional information leads only to delayed emotional involvement. Lawyers who ignore appropriate emotional engagement at the appropriate time– i.e. the time of occurrence, the time for defense– and practice betrayal instead of client defense come to suffer their own emotional problems in the course of time.

In fact, it is the avoidance of appropriate involvement– as in understanding the client's needs and applying Legal System 1– and the myth of objectivity in law that have led to our dysfunctional legal system, preventing lawyers from being good lawyers. Keeping an emotional distance from a client is an objective strategy only to the extent that a lawyer is capable of maintaining a state of denial of emotions, a task that becomes harder with time. A cardinal rule in maintaining general mental health for anyone is that emotional information should be kept up to date. Disagreeable, anxiety-causing information should be processed, not ignored and stored away. The legal system encourages the opposite. 'An innocent man went to prison because you didn't do your job? Stop thinking about it. Life is tough for everybody.'

Reading the law as intended by Legal System 1 can be an inspirational, uplifting experience associated with pride in being a lawyer. The play, *A Man for All Seasons* comes to mind: "This country is planted thick with laws, from coast to coast, Man's laws, not God's! And if you cut them down, and you're just the man to do it, do you really think you could stand upright in the winds that would blow then?"

It makes society feel secure and in good hands to know our justice system can work well. No doubt, many fine young men and women begin the study of law in this light. The bad lawyer and Legal System 2 pervert fine intent and the justifiable expectations for all of us. In that sense it isn't just the bad lawyer's client that is in line for betrayal, but all of society.

THE PSYCHOLOGY OF BETRAYAL

Paul Ricoeur, the French philosopher, pointed out that the tragedy of any evil is not in the act committed, but in the experience of the victim. Betrayal represents a dire alteration of a justifiably presumed, projected future for a victim. The experience of the victim in professional legal relationships, however, is permitted to be defined by the lawyer.

Betrayal is usually mediated by the use of false language, a circumstance that turns out to have a profound, negative impact on the human mind. It is different in quality from, yet no less severe than physical abuse. Emotional pain and harm can last the course of a life and impact future relationships profoundly. It is not unusual for a victim of betrayal to express the thought that even intense physical pain would have been preferable to the experience of emotional betrayal. Indeed, it is certainly not unheard of that people will turn the experience of emotional pain in their lives into intentional physical pain, e.g. cutting themselves, the distraction of physical pain possibly being preferred.

Ask someone for an example of evil today and they will often reflexively refer to the German concentration camps. Auschwitz etc. were clearly evil. Few would disagree, but rare is the person who experiences evil in such an extreme form. I suggest a different, more utilitarian concept of evil for everyday application. Average people experience evil in their lives in the form of deception and betrayal that is mediated by misleading words, in other words... by language. As Napoleon's chief diplomat, Charles Maurice de Tallyrand, observed, "Language was invented so that people could conceal their thoughts from one another." It is language that leads to expectations, and expectations lead to extraordinary thoughts.

Some time ago the *New York Daily News* reported a case in which a Virginia Tech student was sentenced to 45 years in prison for killing her lover. The murderer explained that her lover met her for a date wearing sweatpants while she wore formal dress. Upon realizing that her lover hadn't taken the date seriously, the woman became incensed and ... killed her. Of course, it wasn't the sweatpants that were offensive, but rather the violation of an expectation.

Although the above is an extreme case, everyone is familiar with the pain associated with disappointment and violation of expectations. In the same way, expecting that a lawyer will defend one's innocence, and then to have that expectation betrayed after financial and enormous emotional investment, can be devastating.

To understand the essence of betrayal, consider a toddler who has just been offered a colorful toy. The toddler smiles and reaches for the offering, but it is suddenly withdrawn. A blank look of disappointment ascends and replaces the smile. The toy is again offered and again withdrawn just before it is about to be grasped. Repeated enough times, emotional fatigue sets in. The toddler gives up. Trust is gone. Betrayal exhausts the human brain, rendering it more pliable to suggestion and imposed beliefs.

Words are the most common vehicle to betrayal for those older than toddlers, and words are the lawyer's highly effective weapons. Expecting that a lawyer will defend a client's innocence– an expectation fueled by lawyer words– but encountering betrayal unleashes powerful client emotions that must then be contained within the legal framework.

What might we think of the type of individual who would engage in the above, described activity with a toddler or a child … or anyone? Sadistic perhaps? Power-hungry to a pathetic level? How many people would engage in the above, described activity, then wish to have it filmed and released on the internet? Chances are that some individuals might engage in such activity, but no one would wish it to be known to anyone else. They would no doubt like such behavior to be seen as "private" and to be kept "confidential."

The needy client is the child to the powerful lawyer. Yet the exact same tactic as described above and modified can be used privately and kept confidential through lawyer abuse of power in his office. Instead of a colorful toy, the lawyer uses the tease of freedom and vindication, advanced and withdrawn as many times as he wishes to exhaust a client and to achieve a plea bargain.

Betrayal sets off a chain of distressing events in the human brain. This is due to psychological stress, which makes a breakdown of previously held beliefs and expectations necessary to reduce tension. Beliefs are etched physically into a brain in the form of neural networks or brain pathways through a system of interacting brain structures called the limbic system. The limbic system determines what an individual should expect from incoming information. It bases the expectation on past experience, then it informs other parts of the brain, including the cerebral cortex, the seat of consciousness. Our cultural narrative, our strongest beliefs, and our expectations all reach consciousness through the filter of these established neural networks.

The lawyer who relies on betrayal counts fundamentally on the client's pre-existing beliefs and expectations. The expectations come from the legal myth as taught by the culture. He reinforces the myth as he emphasizes Legal System 1, the client's right to justice and a trial etc. When the expectations are dashed, confusion and distress result. The more intense the expectations that are raised and the greater is the need to prove innocence, the greater the impact of client betrayal and the rollover.

Betrayal destroys beliefs embedded in neural networks and therefore it necessitates neural network remodeling to go on with life. The firmer a previously held belief or expectation, the greater the remodeling that becomes necessary. When a client has been betrayed, he will naturally and normally suffer temporary mental destabilization as the required remodeling takes place, bringing neural networks up to date with a new belief system. This, in turn, can provide the bad lawyer with valid reason to claim that a betrayed client is mentally unbalanced.

The false narrative of American justice represents a powerful, determinative set of beliefs, but also a very dangerous set of beliefs because they can profoundly mislead a believer. An important task of this book is to destroy the false narrative of what to expect from the justice system and replace it with a healthier and realistic mistrust.

One of many misleading beliefs that is emphatically pronounced at the start of a professional relationship with a lawyer is that the client should trust him completely. That trust, however, is put forth in reference to lawyer-client confidentiality, which has its very practical limits. Lawyers know these limits but the client does not. While the concept of lawyer-client confidentiality may seem reassuring to a client, it actually offers no protection from lawyer betrayal. In fact, confidentiality can come to aid a lawyer in concealing his wrongdoing with a client.

In a case in Wisconsin in which a lawyer promised strict confidentiality regarding personal information revealed in his office, the lawyer later agreed to an in camera hearing, with the judge and others present, when the prosecutor suspected the existence of the information. This breach of confidentiality was explained to the client as simply one exception to the rule. Similarly, a tax lawyer in Wisconsin promised confidentiality regarding the disclosure of financial information, but yielded immediately when pressed by an opposing lawyer. The tax lawyer later explained sheepishly, "I didn't think that the judge would allow that."

THE NERVOUS SYSTEM AND BETRAYAL

A client's susceptibility to lawyer manipulations, deceit and betrayal depends on his ability to withstand the imposed psychological stresses. The eminent 20th century Russian physiologist, Ivan Pavlov, who studied the physiology of dogs extensively, concluded that, just like dogs, we humans also exhibit four types of nervous systems in relation to stress. These range from labile to stable, or what we might consider simply as from weak to strong.

The type of nervous system that a dog or a person exhibits determines how much stimulation must be applied before specific, engrained behavioral traits (or in the case of humans, beliefs) are extinguished. For example, a dog with a labile nervous system requires less stimulation to extinguish the learned response of expecting food when a bell rings than does a dog with a stable nervous system. In the context of lawyer coercion for a plea bargain, the 'stimulation' applied by the lawyer would arise from the tools of lawyer betrayal as already mentioned. The 'engrained trait' to be extinguished in the case of an innocent client is his will to continue claiming innocence.

MARK INGLIN

Nature provides a range of nervous systems among organisms as a response to differing genetics and environments. Both 'weak and 'strong' nervous systems have their specific advantages or disadvantages at different times and in different environments. Individuals therefore range from being more or less susceptible to psychological manipulation through the application of psychological stressors. In the environment of the innocent client and the bad lawyer, the more labile nervous system is at a great disadvantage. People who have this type of nervous system plea bargain quickly, guilty or not. Their nervous systems are readily stimulated and their beliefs changed to suit the lawyer who imposed the stress, followed by the new belief.

Some individuals can withstand stress for a long time before they become emotionally exhausted, others simply cannot. The evil of the legal system in the form of Legal System 2 resides in the fact that it equates the susceptibility of an accused individual (with a labile or stable nervous system) to imposed stress with the guilt or innocence of that individual. It does this intentionally, as it permits lawyers to use psychological tools, privately and confidentially, to separate people into weak or strong categories. District attorneys certainly do not raise objection to this winnowing; they welcome it.

And who among us might the 'weak' individuals be? The poor? The passive? The poets? The artists? The formerly abused? The generally sensitive and intellectually unfortunate? This willingness to abandon the weak to their fate is a reflection of an animal nature by which worthiness is measured only by resistance to adversity and raw domination. It obviously should have nothing to do with justice.

An analysis of how our legal system disrespects innocence and permits Legal System 2 to operate so widely must inevitably lead to the conclusion that primal satisfaction is more important than rational considerations in our justice system. Bad lawyers are routinely permitted to break-down individuals emotionally using Legal System 2, then to label them as guilty in Legal System 1. That is why we have the ninety-five percent statistic on plea bargains. The fact that this is allowed to happen with a remarkable degree of complacency (although things seem to be heading in a more positive direction, thanks to fine journalism) points to our value system. We value the tough, resistant and resilient nervous system above the innocence of the innocent individual. This is also reflected in our love of the mobster, the tough-guy, the strong-man image and the blind eye that we turn to the brutality among the police.

An outstanding example of the above comes from a Swiss district attorney who allowed criminal suspects to be subjected to psychological manipulation during interrogations, to the degree of staging a kabuki-like mini-drama in the interrogation room. His office permits interrogations complete with characters who arrive and depart the interrogation room without introduction, playing parts that contribute to an air of mystery and anxiety. After thereby arousing anxiety, the interrogating detective reaches dramatically behind his chair for a thick tome on a shelf, purportedly defining the suspect's crime to a tee. He raises his voice and booms his accusation: "You see, this book shows it here, you are guilty."

Some individuals break emotionally and a crime has been solved. The dramatic gestures can have no purpose other than to test whether a suspect possesses a nervous system strong enough to withstand the stress. If he does not, he is guilty. The process is logically equivalent to expecting Swiss cows to pee fondue.

A client in the hands of a bad lawyer is an open invitation to abuse that induces any number of negative psychological effects in the client. For example, following the defeat of a claim of innocence a client can be expected to suffer from the so-called "loser effect." Failure following the opposite expectation (derived from lawyer promises) saps a person's confidence and makes him feel resigned and hopeless, triggering a downward emotional spiral. In addition, outsiders may then shun the failed individual in what is called the "reverse-halo effect." If we see a person as having negative characteristics in one light, e.g. a loser for failing to demonstrate his innocence in the legal system, we will often see them as failures in completely unrelated ways.

The loser effect and a downward emotional spiral decrease the chances that a betrayed client will be able to fight-on or fight back when betrayed by his lawyer. As a loser, a complaint made about a lawyer will appear feeble– sour grapes and nothing more. But a client who succumbs to unethical manipulation also has an insidious effect on the lawyer himself. He enjoys one more success gained unethically. That is, while a lawyer may convince himself at the start of a professional relationship that he will defend an innocent client, his own past and mounting history of deceit will undermine his ability to do so. The lawyer will literally reach a point at which he feels unease at the thought of providing full support for any client and winning any case. The lawyer also becomes a loser, a complacent loser. As he diminishes his efforts with any client he justifies this by claiming that the client no longer fulfilled his criteria for worthy defense. In fact, it is the lawyer's evolved 'feelings' about his client that are rationalized, becoming the basis for his inadequate defense. A lack of empathy grips the lawyer and he uses his power to rid himself of the annoying feeling. The cycle begins anew with each new client.

THE *LAWYER BETRAYAL SYNDROME*

In an article entitled "Why Do People Stay in Abusive Relationships," Harvard Medical School abuse expert Dr. Craig Malkin explains that individuals under emotional or physical abuse come to suffer dissociation or detachment from the reality of the abuse. "Dissociating victims cannot leave the abuse because they aren't psychologically present enough to recall the pain of what happened," Malkin explains.

Victims of dissociation come under the influence of their abusers; they view their abuse as normal. As a result, they make no effort to combat or change their situation. Privacy, intimacy and circumstances that permit any type of abuse– verbal, physical or emotional– can alter perspective and minimize the perception of abuse by a victim. Domestic violence, indoctrination by cults and fanatical religious groups represent typical circumstances in which the dynamic of domination and dissociation is exhibited between abusers and victims.

In the eyes of an abuser, the success of his abuse arises from the dissociation, which he interprets as tacit approval given by the victim for the abuse. This teaches the abuser that the abuse should continue, because it maintains the victim's inability to object. At the same time, abuse can strengthen a perverse, negative emotional bond between the abuser and the victim. Expectations of success via abuse can be firmly established and reinforced over time. Once an abuser is finally overthrown by a victim, however, the perpetrator can disintegrate with catastrophic results, including suicide.

To my knowledge, until now, no one has implicated the legal profession in generally abusive behavior or has compared its members to classical abusers, or compared legal clients to classical abuse victims. Yet evidence points in that direction. It is highly unlikely that the criminal justice system could enjoy a ninety-five percent clearance rate as a result of innocent clients changing their minds of their own, free will. It is far more likely that we have a systemic problem that we are not willing to see– much like the situation with the Catholic clergy abuse of the weak and innocent that lasted for decades– or that we fear revealing for what it actually is.

LAWYERS BROKEN BAD

In introducing the term *Lawyer Betrayal Syndrome* (LBS), the intent here is to raise awareness among legal clients who may have been betrayed, that they could well be classical victims of abuse and, if so, their reactions to lawyer betrayal are normal responses to abuse.

Any notion that a betrayed legal client should have left his offending lawyer should be dispelled. The responsibility for unethical or illegal conduct does not rest with a client-victim, any more than it does with an abused child or a classic adult abuse victim. The victim of a coercive lawyer should not be placed in a position of defending his behavior when manipulated by a legal professional. Understanding the *Lawyer Betrayal Syndrome* will help betrayed clients and their loved ones comprehend the psychological processes that lead to mental anguish due to betrayal by their own lawyers. It will also warn potential legal clients of the possible dangers in a defense lawyer's office.

The *Lawyer Betrayal Syndrome* refers to psychological symptoms and behavioral manifestations associated directly with the betrayal of a client in the context of legal representation. It is analogous to the known Stockholm Syndrome and is a subcategory of general betrayal trauma. Whereas the Stockholm Syndrome is defined as an emotional attachment to one's captor in a hostage situation as a result of stress, dependence, and a need to cooperate for survival, LBS is the emotional attachment of a client to his criminal defense lawyer. The attachment forms due to the need to trust the lawyer, the development of dependency, imposed emotional stress and a long-term, unavoidable need to cooperate with the lawyer for vigorous legal defense in the threatening environment of a punitive legal system. Prevailing in a claim of innocence represents existential survival to a client; it is a fundamental need for any innocent person accused of a crime that he did not commit.

A victim of LBS regresses psychologically to a stage of uncertainty and moral confusion. Previously held values and beliefs have been disrupted and weakened. The authority figure, the lawyer, has imposed his values. At the same time, paradoxical feelings of empathy can arises toward the betraying lawyer, as is well known from the Stockholm Syndrome.

The sense of hopefulness and optimism that initially prevailed via the defense lawyer's encouraging words are replaced by insecurity and feelings of worthlessness after the abrupt dissolution of the strongly held belief of promised legal defense in the client rollover. As the victim adopts the values of the betrayer (the imposed conditions of the plea bargain), the sense of isolation, alienation and threat is temporarily eliminated. In Freudian terms, threat and trauma have led a victim to identify with his betrayer, the lawyer, as a means of ego self-defense.

Betrayed legal clients can exhibit signs of psychological distress such as anxiety attacks, and the classic symptoms of post-traumatic stress. The severity of the symptoms depend on the nature and the past experiences of the client's nervous system and factors such as the extent of the client's trust in his lawyer, the tools of betrayal that were used, and the consequence to the client of any failure to prevail in a claim of innocence.

In severe cases of betrayal a "learned helplessness" takes over, as the client becomes exhausted mentally and gives up his own defense completely and stops caring about outcomes in general. The fact that the lawyer contributed to such conditions by unethical conduct is widely disregarded by the legal system. The true lawyer-client history can be kept well-wrapped in the misuse of lawyer-client confidentiality. Any disclosure of the diabolical, step-wise retreat from the lawyer's initial support and encouragement– i.e. his sales pitch to gain a contract– followed by undermining the client and finally to client rollover remains obfuscated. Professional wrongdoing is unlikely to emerge. The legal profession guards against disclosing the tools that force what it rationalizes as the necessary plea bargain.

If a client retains the stamina to register an official complaint against his own lawyer for unethical conduct after being betrayed by a lawyer, the lawyer can point to and exploit the client's 'poor psychological state' in his own defense. Anyway, who will listen and react with effect to a client's complaints about his lawyer's unethical conduct? While legal appeals are certainly available, they are expensive and require great effort. In the case of lawyer' professional failures in any earlier legal procedure or at a trial, it is difficult to find another lawyer courageous enough to expose wrongdoing or negligence by a fellow lawyer.

How many lawyers wish that their powers within the legal system were more limited with regard to their conduct with clients? The legal community has not shown any effort to prevent the emotional abuse of clients by welcoming complaints and investigating them closely, or even to openly admit to or discuss the problem. The client therefore has limited options for meaningful recourse.

The weakening of the victim's will to challenge the very person who initiates the betrayal reinforces the use of coercion as a tool to force settlements. This enables bad lawyers to find an easy road to financial and career success. LBS can thus be viewed as the outcome to a form of lawyer 'success.' The success leads to a positive feedback loop, encouraging the same strategy to be used on the next client and surely noted by other lawyers. In this regard, we see that "normalization of deviance," the creeping tolerance away from standards of ethics to the point of complete system failure. In the American system of justice that point has been reached.

Oscar Wilde famously stated that every profession is a conspiracy against the layman. This may be true of the legal profession more than for any other profession. While every other profession is subject to oversight by lawyers when all other remedies have failed, the legal system, when practiced as Legal System 2, holds itself exempt from corrective oversight.

PART 4

FAILURES OF OVERSIGHT

IN SHREVEPORT, LOUISIANA in 1983, Glenn Ford was accused of robbing and murdering his employer, a local jeweler. His prosecutor, 32-year-old Marty Stroud, convicted him based on the fact that Ford was working for the victim and also had a history of petty theft. No evidence other than Ford's past misdemeanors was presented. Ford became one of the longest death row occupants, serving thirty years in prison.

Stroud continued in a successful legal career, but three decades later a man named Jake Robinson confessed to killing the jeweler. The court subsequently found it likely that Ford was neither present nor had he participated in the crime. On hearing the news, Stroud recalled, "I thought I was going to throw up. I felt my face was just burning, like a fever from the horror of knowing that yours truly had caused him all of this pain."

At the trial, no physical evidence had linked Ford to the crime. The main witness admitted that she had been coerced by police to fabricate her testimony. "We excluded African Americans because we felt that they would not consider a death penalty where you had a black defendant and a white victim," Stroud explained as he took responsibility for the decision.

The above account was extracted from a CBS 60 Minutes broadcast. In the interview, with CBS, Stroud explained how the culture of winning clouded his ability to perform his job properly: "I was arrogant, narcissistic, caught up in the culture of winning. ... Looking back on it, there was a question of other people's involvement. I should have followed up on that. I didn't." When asked by the interviewer why he hadn't followed-up, Stroud responded, "I think my failure to say something can only be described as cowardice. I was a coward."

To be a coward means to be afraid, thereby acting inappropriately in some expected way. What, exactly, was Stroud afraid of? As argued here, lawyers fear offending other members of the legal system and the local law enforcement community. They also fear career failure. As there is no effective oversight that applies pressure in favor of ethical conduct, based on simple, human nature the prosecutor who avoids acting unethically may be the exception. Stroud knew– as every prosecutor does– that a conviction would enhance his career. He had the power to do just that at the expense of another human being with less power.

Today, former prosecutor Stroud admits that the system was rigged against the accused. Ford's court-appointed lawyer never practiced criminal law; he had instead practiced law in the area of wills and estates. If a general medical practitioner performs brain surgery and the patient dies, lawyers will line up to claim gross negligence and collect for their client. But the legal system shields itself from such accountability. There is no other profession in which an unqualified professional can replace a qualified professional, such as in the example above, and not be held responsible.

The current district attorney, Dale Cox, however, sees things quite differently. In his view, no one did anything wrong. "I think he has gotten delayed justice," Cox explained, "The system did not fail Mr. Ford." Regarding the unfairness of thirty years in prison for a crime he did not commit, Cox says dismissively, "It's better than dying there and it's better than being executed."

For his part, Ford was entitled to $330,000, or $11,000 for each year of incarceration, but the State denied him the money on a legal technicality. When Cox was asked whether he felt this was unfair, he responded by saying, "No, I think we need to follow the law." Ford was granted a $20 gift certificate upon leaving Angola prison. It read, "Wish you luck." He died penniless.

When Cox was asked about room for compassion in such a case, he remarked, "I am not in the compassion business, none of us as prosecutors or defense lawyers are in the compassion business. I think the ministry is in the compassion business. We are in the legal business. So to suggest that somehow what has happened to Glenn Ford is abhorrent, yes, it's unfair. But it's not illegal. And it's not even immoral. It just doesn't fit your perception of fairness."

Dale Cox, in his statements, all but establishes by name the existence of Legal System 1 and Legal System 2 as defined in this book. The rules for lawyers are fuzzy; they permit shifting between the two systems depending on the needs of a legal professional to squirm away from responsibility. In his view, a thirty-year delay of justice remains within the parameters of Legal System 1, regardless of the fact that Legal System 2 took its place long ago and for all those years. The bait and switch between Legal Systems 1 and 2, as so often happens, was fully consummated and then put on display in this particular case. For years, a man was claimed to be guilty under the societal cover and righteousness of Legal System 1, but all long it was Legal System 2 at work.

One can scarcely imagine an individual in any other profession, industry, or line of work getting away with the above level of gross reconstruction of what is fair and moral. Such outrageous public defense of obvious dysfunction would be thought of as mental pathology– a level of denial close to anosognosia– followed by the removal of that person from a position of public responsibility. But a 'hard ass' legal mentality, with power (and testosterone) as its drug of choice and denial its weapon, is widely accepted and often admired. The notion of 'strong and wrong' has greater emotional appeal than 'weak and right.' This constitutes a great paradox, as it belies the prevailing myth of the objectivity of law. Denial of wrongdoing is readily tolerated within the legal system because it affords protection for everyone in the system, sometimes retroactively and for years. 'One day, it is you who may need protection, for your error.' No other profession but the legal profession has such protection readily at hand for its members.

In New Zealand, I had the opportunity to interview a prosecutor along the lines of Mr. Stroud. I asked him how he felt when he discovered that an innocent person went to prison not because of guilt, but because of ineffective assistance of counsel. "Well, he answered, "you can't even begin to think about that." He then went on to explain how the courtroom was his battlefield (the metaphor of choice among lawyers) and his job, indeed, was to win.

In a case demonstrating failure of oversight, a client who registered a complaint through the board of attorneys' professional responsibilities against a prominent criminal defense lawyer in Wisconsin waited months before the board responded. It finally stated in a letter that its investigation revealed no misconduct on the part of the lawyer. Incredulous, the client asked to examine the nature of the claimed investigation by the board. A response several weeks later contained a half-page letter from the accused lawyer merely refuting all of the detailed accusations. The lawyer's letter in his own defense represented the entire "investigation" undertaken by the board.

The client subsequently questioned the board for its use of the term "investigation" for the submission of a half-page letter from the accused lawyer, and he demanded action. Months passed; an embarrassed board responded positively by recognizing and itemizing suspected professional violations by the lawyer. It assigned a special agent, another lawyer in that community, to investigate. Close to a year passed before the client finally received a letter from the investigating lawyer, stating that he had just now come to realize that he had a conflict of interest, as he had worked on cases together with the accused lawyer. A new investigating lawyer would need to be appointed … .

The overall problem with the legal system always traces back to the extreme imbalances of power, especially between the prosecution, with its freedom to load charge sheets excessively and to improperly conceal evidence, and the defense lawyer, who can be rendered feeble by lack of courage brought about by concerns for his career in a punitive local legal community. But as Frank Serpico, the idealistic New York police officer who refused to accept bribes and who was portrayed in the movie *Serpico*, said, as long as good cops are more afraid of bad cops than the law, there will be police corruption. The same principle holds true for lawyers.

In her book *10-10-10*, author Suzy Welch suggests that we should distinguish between the wisdom of decisions that are made considering where our lives will be in 10-minutes versus 10-months versus 10-years. The legal system uniquely allows a decision made by a lawyer in consideration of his next ten minutes to prevail for years by force of stubbornness and denial, as in the case of Glenn Ford. While prosecutor Stroud commendably tried to make amends personally, *de facto* the system defended a bad '10-minute' decision even thirty years later.

When accused of impropriety, no one is better suited to defend himself than a lawyer. Not only is the lawyer an insider (he has relationships to count on), he knows how to interpret the law as Legal System 1 to his advantage. An accused lawyer will know secrets and misdeeds on the parts of colleagues; these can be used to blunt the exposure of evidence and criticism using Legal System 2. If a lawyer finds himself under investigation, he can resort to stalling and denial that can go on for years, incurring exorbitant costs and imposing mental exhaustion on an average client. The only person with little need to fear the phrase, "I'll call a lawyer" is another lawyer.

Not only are lawyers often exempted from scrutiny, but people with whom they work are also often given a pass from accountability and professionalism. Clerks, paralegals, and secretaries rank among the circle of people a lawyer avoids offending. In one case in New Zealand, a clerk provided an incorrect court account number to the family of a defendant who was granted bail. A condition imposed by the judge had been that the funds reach court before the defendant's release from jail. The error entailed considerable inconvenience for a number of people awaiting the defendant's release, not to mention the defendant. The clerk, however, faced no criticism for his error, as the lawyer explained: "It was negligence on the clerk's part that caused this trouble; he should have double-checked the correct account number. But I can't complain about it. This is my home turf. I need these people to remain happy with me." Client "happiness" was of lesser concern.

In theory, lawyer regulatory boards are meant to oversee lawyer conduct and should hold lawyers responsible for any malpractice. However, lawyer malpractice is practically impossible to prove and is rarely punished. The anger of accusation by a client often dissipates in frustration at the slow-cooker obfuscation of the legal system. Accusations tend to go away if enough roadblocks arise. It is in the interest of many parties in the legal system to see that a colleague prevails when he is accused of wrongdoing. An accusing client, on the other hand, has fewer powerful friends, many of whom will advise, 'Let it go and move on with your life.'

In a case in New Zealand, a lawyer forged a power of attorney by extending its expiration date. She then used the forged document to coerce a Swiss bank into transferring a quarter-million dollars from a client's account to hers, falsely claiming an emergency situation had arisen and that the client had approved the transfer. When the client discovered the fraud, he contacted the district attorney in a Swiss jurisdiction. An arrest warrant was issued for bank fraud against the New Zealand lawyer. The Auckland law society where the lawyer practiced was informed of the circumstances and of the arrest warrant, but no action was taken in New Zealand against the lawyer, who continues to practice in the Auckland area in real estate law, despite an arrest warrant issued for bank fraud in Europe.

In his book *The Power Paradox*, Berkeley Professor Dacher Keltner explains that, "True power requires modesty and empathy, not force and coercion. But what people want from leaders–social intelligence– is what is actually damaged by the experience of having gained power."

Keltner's neuroscience research shows that people with power tend to behave like patients who have damaged orbitofrontal lobes– the region of the brain right behind the eye sockets that is responsible for cognition and decision making– a condition that seems to cause impulsive and insensitive behavior. While "modesty and empathy" may be the last thing that we expect from lawyers and prosecutors, the common occurrence of "lies and coercion" would seem to confirm some mental damage resulting from a toxic legal environment and unaccountable power.

Once legal wrongdoing is exposed, responsibility rests with a public that either accepts or rejects such conduct. When informed, of course, many people do sound outrage. Unfortunately there are also many who believe that 'hard-ass' individuals are necessary to protect society from the bad guys. In that view, mistakes by the justice system, especially by police, need to be tolerated so that the guardians of our security are not restricted by rules or limits placed on them. While the 'hard-ass' approach claims to ensure that fewer criminals go free, the question of how many innocent victims suffer wrongful convictions is not addressed.

In the field of economics, the concept of an opportunity cost describes the cost associated with taking one, particular action as compared to not taking alternative options. In the legal system one comparison that should be made is between the cost associated with finding an innocent person guilty and the cost of allowing a guilty person to go free. Because the threat posed by admitting error is so great in a legal system, where power and fear demand that the most serious wrongdoing be concealed, opportunity costs are likely to be enormous for individuals and for society. For example, a man named Michael Morton spent 25 years in prison for a murder that he did not commit, while the real murdered remained free and committed at least one other murder. How would such a cost differential even be calculated? Yet the legal system players responsible were not held to account.

I am not aware of any opportunity cost analyses having been done for any choices made in the legal system. Obviously, they would be virtually impossible to calculate. But by inductive reasoning alone, as with Michael Morton, we know that society is paying a very high price to keep lawyers justifying high law school tuitions.

ADMITTING ERROR

In his book *Do No Harm* the prominent neurosurgeon and pioneer of awake brain cancer surgery, Dr. Henry Marsh, writes, "To admit failure, to admit weakness, you actually have to be very strong.... The important thing is that we all learn from mistakes; we don't learn from our successes."

For members in the legal profession, not only is admitting one's own mistakes frightening, but to hold others in the profession accountable for their mistakes is professional suicide. Admitting to mistakes in the legal system requires exposing the wrongdoing or errors of those within the system, for example errors by the police. The analogy of 'pulling on the thread' is apt here. Once a thread comes undone, pulling on it threatens to unravel the entire fabric. That is not easily undertaken when interdependent, long-term relationships exist and the consequences of wrongdoing are not only the end of a career, but also severe punishment and possibly prison.

Pulling on the thread is a problem throughout the legal system. An article in the *New Yorker* magazine by Nicholas Schmidle titled "Crime Fiction" unfortunately is not fiction and explains the problem perfectly, as below:

In Cook County, Illinois, Craig Futterman, a law professor at the University of Chicago, revealed that exposing the state's attorney office's practice of "consistently standing behind shaky convictions"– even those he described as a "shame and stain" on the city– could unravel decades of wrongful convictions. The office resisted rigorous reviews of particular cases for reasons that could be called "economic," with a consideration of the potential financial liabilities of exposing wrongdoing, and also "relationship issues" that stemmed from heavy reliance on police testimony. If in-house abusive practices were investigated, they could undermine hundreds of felony convictions that relied on the word of crooked detectives, triggering a cascade of overturned verdicts.

"If an individual police officer is exposed, how many other criminal cases might that undermine?" Futterman asks, "If you have a proven instance where an officer lied to put an innocent person in jail, it calls into question all the other cases in which his word has been a primary source of information."

One reason errors go unexplored in the legal system is because there may be no end to culpability and anguish. "Relationship issues" are highly significant for more than just the police. With one eye on career and one on the effect on cronies, the lawyer loses sight of his client and is ever engaged in a balancing act that limits the defense of his client and avoids pulling on the thread. Few lawyers will discuss this problem with a client, however. Moreover, to accuse and hold someone accountable, cooperation will be necessary among powerful, influential, legally skilled entities– i.e. other lawyers. A lawyer who goes up against another lawyer may need to continue working in the accused lawyer's community with the very people who may have reason to value practical outcome over theoretical law.

A prosecutor in Milwaukee deliberately lied to a jury on the extensive, official legal history of a case; he also helped police conceal exculpatory evidence. The defense lawyer colluded with the prosecutor, as both had an interest in protecting the legal community and police from criticism. At sentencing, the prosecutor emphasized, in open court for all to hear, that "no other jurisdiction must ever be allowed to examine this case."

This prosecutor practically admitted that he had rigged a trial and that he had violated legal ethics and the law, but within his own *jursdiction. He also knew that legal practitioners in another jurisdiction would recognize the violations in an instant, while local 'geography' had forced his hand in the direction of betraying his professional duty, but could be relied on to conceal the misconduct.*

Switzerland is no different from the USA in regard to lawyers bowing to local politics for the sake of career. One Swiss lawyer, questioned on the extent to which he would engage in defense of his client, answered, "Obviously, I am not going to disrupt the local power structure if it means harming my future. I have a family. But a client has the option of going to the next town; surely he will find a lawyer there who will not be influenced by the limitation that I have in my community."

This Swiss lawyer was simply stating his perception of the impossibility of applying Legal System 1 for certain clients, due to local politics. What if a client can't find, or is restricted from finding, a lawyer who will provide adequate defense in another geographical location? There is no need for courage if the battle can be staged far away from the soldier.

Because legal practitioners practically have no means to absolve themselves of guilt for using Legal System 2, their deeds often twist inside themselves with inevitable outward manifestations. Oblique references to personally harbored guilt abound aplenty with lawyers, if you look for them. In psychological terms the phenomenon of projecting outwardly the transgressions not admitted to oneself is known as acting through "the disowned self." For example, the prosecutor in the above example had no rational reason to explain to a courtroom full of people that another jurisdiction must not be allowed to examine a case that he had just rigged. Earlier, we had the example of a judge who confessed in open court that he should probably not punish a defendant for having demanded a trial, but then punished him anyway for having taken the court's time. And I have heard a Milwaukee lawyer explain to a group of people how his recent selection of an all-white jury, which he had masterminded, had ensured that his client, who had information detrimental to his colleagues, would not prevail.

In contrast to the denials, cover-ups and irrational defenses that we hear when wrongdoing is exposed to the public in the legal system, there is one, major American industry in which the exact opposite approach has been taken. In the U.S. commercial aviation industry an employee is guaranteed safety and security if he comes forth with errors, his own as well as those of others. A strict policy of no retribution for admitted error applies. However, an employee is subject to punishment or dismissal if he withholds knowledge of error. The result of this policy is an exemplary safety record for aviation in the United States.

Applying the approach taken by commercial aviation to the admission of error to our legal system is difficult to imagine. A massive shift in the culture would be required. Such shifts have taken place in other countries on related issues, however. For example, Britain and Canada have changed their systems of criminal interrogation away from accusation and threats– as exemplified by what is called the Reid technique of interrogation, as practiced in the USA and in Switzerland– over to the PEACE (Preparation and Planning, Engage and Explain, Account, Closure and Evaluate) method of interrogation, which is intended purely to determine only the facts of a case. The result has been fewer false confessions and more actual criminals being held responsible.

The PEACE method leaves no room for cowboy-style interrogators, prejudices and superstitions, or the induction of fear by detectives who wish to solve crimes by intimidating an accused individual who happens to have a labile nervous system. It seeks facts in a deliberately relaxed, non-threatening atmosphere. A fact-finding-only approach in the criminal justice system would require individuals to relinquish power, mainly over the accused, the weakest links. It would require an end to impulsivity and false intuition about who is guilty and who is not. However, status quo bias, one of the strongest impulses in human nature and a cornerstone of tribal cohesion, would provide stiff resistance to any such change.

The medical profession offers another example of an association with ethical and economic interests that is moving forward on the admission of errors by its members. Medical practitioners are terrified of having legal action taken against them, which can lead to expensive settlements and the threat of professional ruin. No equivalent motivation exists in the legal system to elevate lawyer standards. In the case of medical error, there is a growing emphasis on exposing errors in a blame-free environment in order to prevent future occurrences. For example, at Virginia Mason

Hospital, a top facility in Seattle, the hospital takes a three-step approach following a medical error: 1) admit the error; 2) have someone responsible step forward; 3) make a meaningful apology.

It has now been found that the admission of mistakes in the medical field leads to better outcomes for everyone and smaller financial settlements or no legal action at all. There is no discussion of such an effort in the legal system. This is not because lawyers by their nature are fundamentally any different from professionals in other areas, but rather because the oversight that they provide for other professions is entirely lacking for their own. Lawyers are not eager to limit their own powers. There is no incentive to root around looking for problems in the legal system. The question of 'Well, what are they going to do to me?' following wrongdoing by a legal profession includes little if any fear of repercussions or punishment. The environment, after all, is responsible for the nature of its inhabitants.

Recently, the New York Times reported that a federal judge in Texas was so disturbed by the lack of truthfulness by U.S. Department of Justice lawyers in his court that he instructed hundreds of them to undergo ethics training. The request came because U.S. District Judge Andrew S. Hanen suspected that Justice Department lawyers intentionally misled him in the course of a lawsuit filed by Texas and other states challenging the Obama administration's immigration policy.

The Department of Justice responded by saying that the ethics training mandated would cost more than $7.8 million, and that the *sanctions ordered by the Court "far exceed the bounds of appropriate remedies for what this Court concluded were intentional misrepresentations, a conclusion that was reached without proper procedural protections and that lacks sufficient evidentiary support."*

With regard to the legal system, Tallyrand was certainly on to something when he explained that the purpose of language is to hide thoughts. Law can turn into an obsessive, neverending game of words devised to mislead and deceive, as lawyers take open pride in their ability to contort words into any meaning. Recall the famous words by President Bill Clinton, a lawyer: "It depends on what the meaning of the word *is* is." By going on to state that "I did not have sexual relations with that woman" he relied on the fuzzy meaning of the term "sexual relations," because fellatio and intimate maneuverings with cigars, technically speaking, are not intercourse.

In the legal system, without afforded scrutiny and the proper raising of ridicule for sheer obfuscation and nonsense, the twisting of words is accepted. Common sense examination by individuals other than lawyers could stop much that is wrong in the legal system. Fear of the system, however, neutralizes both investigation and criticism in average cases, keeping critics at bay, happy to avoid any interactions with the entangling legal system.

On occasion, a lawyer will ask a client to lie for him, if he thinks that his personal or professional interests are at risk. In Wisconsin, where a lawyer was defending a client in a First Amendment case, the lawyer took on the case and accepted the retainer while vigorously proclaiming his intention to defend his client's right to freedom of speech. When the client later sent the lawyer an article he had written for publication containing information on corruption by a local judge, the lawyer instructed his client that, "At the upcoming deposition you will state that you did not send me this article; I never saw it. Do you understand?" Dismayed at the information contained in the article, the lawyer continued, "And I forbid you to ever write anything about me." The lawyer dismissed his own responsibility to defend his client's right to freedom of speech when that speech exposed wrongful conduct by a member of the legal system in the lawyer's community.

Clients often agree to lie because they fear that refusing to follow a lawyer's instructions will put them at legal risk. They could lose lawyer support and thereby be held responsible for their own loss or, worse, simply be abandoned by the lawyer. A client would be transgressing the will of an authority figure who provides a sense of security. If a client does not follow his lawyer's instructions, then he is showing a frightful independence from lawyer strategy. Or is the lawyer actually testing to see just how pliable the client is? In any case, the lawyer never doubts who is responsible for lying, even if he provided the instruction to do so.

Fortunately, fewer people today have faith that our law enforcement and legal institutions are working as they should. This is a good thing. Sad to say, regardless of a legal outcome, it can be argued that a defendant may be better off emotionally, and therefore mentally, if he has no positive expectations of the legal system and does not trust his own lawyer. Jail may be in his future, but psychological afflictions from betrayed trust may be lessened or avoided.

POLICE CRIMES

Prosecutors cannot do their jobs without close cooperation with police. Defense lawyers must interact with prosecutors and thus with police. Police are subject to the same pressures of peer protection and careerism as prosecutors and lawyers. Like prosecutors, they are motivated to achieve career rewards by establishing in court that others– the accused– have done wrong. Police conduct is therefore critical to a valid finding of the guilt or innocence of a lawyer's client.

The idea that 'most cops are good' may be true in isolation, but police do not work in isolation. The salient question is how many cops are 'good' when they are required to disclose information counter to the prosecution or expose fellow police misconduct in determining guilt or innocence. That question has been resoundingly answered, and it is not 'good.'

Illustrative of a problem with police truthfulness and misconduct are recent videos appearing on the internet that, when matched to police reports on the same incident before release of video, show deliberate falsification. One of many such revealing videos concerns the case of Delwran Small, as reported in the *New York Post*. The police officer who shot and killed Small falsified his report of the incident, only to have camera footage show otherwise later.

Police crimes in general are not uncommon. In a report titled "Here's How Often Cops Are Arrested for Breaking the Laws They're Paid to Uphold," reporter Matt Ferner of the *Huffington Post* reveals that 41 percent of total crimes by police are even committed while on duty. In the article, Philip Stinson, the lead researcher in the study and a Bowling Green State University professor, reveals that although they were off-duty, officers committed crimes using the powers granted them as sworn members of law enforcement, or knowledge gained through their authority as police officers. Any distinction between on-or-off duty is thus of little significance. The article went on to note that police officers are reluctant to report misconduct by fellow officers, and some agencies tend not to take seriously any complaints of misconduct, criminal or otherwise. "The process of police socialization and the deep police subculture," Stinson says, "demand further scrutiny... . They just do whatever they want to do because law enforcement is exempt from law enforcement."

The idea that police do what they want to do because they are exempt from law enforcement transmits to lawyers, who feel that police and themselves are exempt from law. As outrageous as it may sound, lawyers and judges often take for granted that police will lie on the witness stand, even under oath at a trial. According to Joe Sexton, senior editor for *Propublica*, "New York City police officers often make false arrests, tamper with evidence and commit perjury on the witness stand."

Police lie because the system in which they work prioritizes their welfare over that of the public. If a police officer accuses his colleagues of lying and unethical behavior, he will not earn points to advance his career, to say the least. In "Why Police Lie under Oath," an article in the *New York Times,* Professor of Law Michelle Alexander states:

> Thousands of people plead guilty to crimes every year in the United States because they know that the odds of a jury's believing their word over a police officer's are slim to none. As a juror, whom are you likely to believe, the alleged criminal in an orange jumpsuit or two well-groomed police officers in uniforms who just swore to God they're telling the truth, the whole truth and nothing but? As one of my colleagues recently put it, 'Everyone knows you have to be crazy to accuse the police of lying.'

The reluctance to voice internal criticism among police derives from the code of silence that governs police practice. There is also a code of lawyer silence, but it is far more difficult to bring to light, and cameras cannot help. Police misconduct is often physical and therefore makes a visceral impression. Lawyer misconduct is emotional and depends on words that usually are not found on the record.

By any rational measure, the tacit acceptance of police lying by agents of the legal system, judges and lawyers should, on its own, render an outcome in a criminal procedure automatically suspect. If police officers were challenged by lawyers for lying under oath. other officers might take notice and their might be improvement. Currently, we have the absurd situation in which no cop is challenged for lying and every lawyer has the excuse of saying, as above, 'I'd have to be crazy to accuse the police of lying,' even though his own client suffers the consequences of his failure of courage. And if it is taken for granted that a defense lawyer will allow a cop to lie in court without serious challenge, what else does the lawyer take for granted as residing out of his proper bounds?

The concept of not even considering certain difficult but ethically-demanded actions because doing so would be 'crazy' only confirms the power of status quo bias. This attitude is surely not limited to that of lawyers allowing police to lie. There are many such tribal rules for lawyers regarding the protection of personalities in their professional circle, other lawyers and judges as the obvious examples.

The culture of silence around police crimes tells us that law enforcement is granted exemptions when it comes to the law because society falls prey to the potential 'barbarians at the gate' threat. A tough cop is permitted to be a crooked cop because society allows conjoining the two with its own protection. Police misconduct tends to be tolerated because we fear they may abandon us, as warnings about this are issued by police spokesmen from time to time. The phenomenon has been known as the "blue flu," an artificial sick-out or work stoppage by police to protest working conditions or criticism. In a well-publicized example, the Santa Clara California Police Officers Association threatened that some of its officers might refuse to patrol a football team's games because a team member had criticized the police and made references to their brutality.

The quick-draw, I-have-the-power mentality, whether involving police or lawyers, is a primal, vestigial reaction that persists because we allow it. It isn't necessary to trade justice for security, but it is certainly easier to do so. Acting first and easy, then thinking hard only later reflects a failure in basic training. Daniel Kahneman, the author of the best-selling book *Thinking Fast and Slow* explains the concept well. Thinking fast is reflexive behavior from our primitive past. Shooting first and asking questions later is one holdover from the early days of mankind, when a rustle in the bushes had to be considered a poisonous snake for the sake of personal survival. Action is taken; regrets can be issued later if it wasn't a snake.

MEDIA AND BIAS

From time to time we see notorious cases on television handled by high-profile lawyers. These cases are extremely rare in comparison to the numbers of criminal cases that pass through the legal system every day, untelevised and unnoted. Only a small fraction of legal cases receive attention other than within a limited, local sphere. But media attention paid to prominent lawyers– F. Lee Bailey, Johnny Cochran types– reinforces unwarranted stereotypes that are counterproductive to a true understanding of our legal system.

The defense will spare no effort! Even the slightest doubt requires acquittal! At high legal expenses per day this may well be true, as with the O. J. Simpson case, but it is misleading to view these examples as representative. They mold our perceptions of the legal system in ways that do not hold in the vast majority of cases. (But in this regard we should also pose a question: Why should a high-powered, high cost lawyer be any better than any other lawyer? Is it knowledge of law that really makes the difference? Hardly. It is the parameters that form the permitted confines of Legal System 2 that elevate lawyers into high-powered status.)

It should be no revelation that being in the spotlight changes human behavior. With media attention, a defense lawyer will put forth the most vigorous defense of a client using Legal System 1, as is his mandate. The environment, however, molds its inhabitants. In star position a lawyer acts the part of a star. With the spotlight off the star fades and local politics again predominate. Patterns of self-interest take over rather than the behavior seen in the exceptions.

The most obvious example of legal misconduct concealed in unpublicized cases is the selection of juries based on skin color, a practice that is clearly illegal. If a case has the national spotlight, the jury in an urban area will be of mixed color for the cameras. But where there is no media attention, improper exclusion of black jurors is business as usual, materializing through the misuse of preemptory challenges and other lawyer/prosecutor subterfuge.

In a case in Wisconsin, a criminal defense lawyer explained to his client that it was important to keep specific 'mindsets' from serving on a jury at certain times, while at other times the same mindsets could be useful. "For example, blacks as a group are ardent supporters of the underdog and will give the benefit of the doubt to a defendant," explained the lawyer, a well-known defender of high profile drug dealers. *This information, he continued, came from a service that polled social groups on their attitudes and opinions and developed behavioral profiles. The profiles help lawyers select juries based on business decisions, not on the intent of the law.*

The abuse of lawyer power isn't necessarily restricted to the privacy of a lawyer's office. Sometimes it takes place right in the courtroom. Lawyers will go to invidious lengths to ensure that a jury is favorable, while making it appear as if its selection had been fair and impartial. In one case in Wisconsin the judge, prosecutor, defense lawyer decided, before a trial and on the official record, that one black juror was eligible for service. As open selection of jurors was announced in the courtroom, his name was not called. Instead, he was substituted by a white juror at the last minute. If anyone checked, the record would show that one, black Mr. X was ruled eligible for service in the discussion on juror eligibility. Looking more closely, they would also see that he was never actually called, replaced instead by a white juror who had not been discussed in chambers. The jury turned out all white in a city one-third African American. No one checked very closely, nor was it expected that anyone would.

The above conduct, like many similar examples in other regards, rarely reaches the public. Legal system players feel secure that their local media will generally permit only established voices to make legally-related pronouncements. Only a lawyer can judge whether black Americans have been wrongfully excluded from a jury, and thus it never happens. The confidence that unfavorable information can be contained traces back to what is known as "access journalism." Established figures in the legal system are in a position to provide information to reporters over the long term. Lone voices have no such influence. If a lone voice offends an established, influential lawyer, for example, that lawyer can cut off the supply of information to the journalist who reports the unfavorable story.

The ultimate source of official information in the legal system, of course, is the court of law and its pronouncements. Like any other institution, however, courts and the judges who staff them must receive scrutiny and have their wrongdoing disclosed to prevent misconduct. But courts and often judges in routine cases enjoy a status of unassailability, especially in local media. Denying that they are populated by fallible human beings adds to the problem of concealment of wrongdoing by lawyers.

An example of undeserved deference to a court of law and a judge was shown by a Swiss politician who received information pointing to corruption at a Swiss university. Rather than investigating the allegations, her response was an automatic, "Let the court decide." The court, however, was strongly biased toward concealing evidence that would have done harm to a local institution and its financial interests.

Not surprisingly, incriminating evidence was then hidden in court with the assistance of the judge. Both the politician and Swiss media were thereby relieved of a burden when the court whitewashed the case.

Trials that are not subject to media or public scrutiny can be dark places where insider rules only apply. In a low-profile case in Wisconsin for which media was not present (and in fact, was actively kept away by an influential lawyer), a defendant was denied the opportunity to present exculpatory evidence and defense witnesses to the jury by his own lawyer (that lawyer had made no provisions for a trial; he had assumed there would be a last-minute plea bargain). Contrary to a firmly established rule by which the prosecution presents its evidence first to the jury, thereby allowing for a concluding rebuttal by the defense, the defense, prosecution and judge agreed in this case to have what amounted to a non-existent defense presented first to the jury. The defendant testified alone, with no backup by defense evidence or witnesses allowed. The prosecution then followed with its case and witnesses in the conclusion to the trial. The prosecutor suggested to the jury that the defendant was mentally ill, which, he implied, explained the lack of witnesses, the lack of defense evidence, and the reverse order of case presentation.

How is it possible that virtually every significant rule established for a fair trial by Legal System 1 was violated in the above case? Ask a law professor about such an occurrence in an American courtroom and he will assure you that this 'cannot happen,' and that, for example, the defense always presents its case to the jury last. While law professors and Legal System 1 say it cannot happen, Legal System 2 winks.

When media are uninterested in or fear reporting a legal case, as in the above, lawyers feel empowered to practice their paternalism. If an average client approaches media with a story of this type, the reaction will be that it 'cannot happen.' We saw this play out perfectly in the movie *Spotlight*, which depicted a true story about the scandal involving pedophile priests and the Catholic Church. A saintly Catholic priest molesting a child 'cannot happen.' The flourishing of misconduct often relates back to the power of simple audacity coupled to the reflex of disbelief.

For journalists as well as lawyers, objectivity may be the mantra, but every journalist is aware of the impact of his reporting on the local community. Blowback in response to what journalists write can emanate from individuals who control their careers. Rarely are the status quo, established relationships, and access to future sources less important than a single, current source of information.

A Swiss journalist working for a major newspaper lamented the fact that, in small Switzerland, the reporting of wrongs committed by individuals at influential institutions is uncomfortable because "you run into those people all the time at the train stations."

No one is foolish enough to imagine that personal relationships have no influence on journalists, but to put revealing the truth at the mercy of encounters at train stations stretches the concept somewhat

LAWYERS BROKEN BAD

too far towards absurdity, especially in a democracy with a reputation for good governance and 'cleanliness.'

In her book, *The Journalist and the Murderer*, author Janet Malcolm writes, "Every journalist who is not too stupid or too full of himself to notice what is going on knows that what he does is indefensible. He is a kind of confidence man preying on people's vanity, ignorance or loneliness, gaining their trust and betraying them without remorse." The bad lawyer, like the bad journalist, is also a confidence man, but one who preys on a client's innate need to defend himself and his innocence.

The journalist may exploit a source improperly and then delude himself into thinking he is printing the truth when, in fact, it has been filtered through the lens of risk or reward to his career. The lawyer does something similar, but he has a more complex and usually closer relationship with a client than a reporter has with a source. The lawyer has more opportunity to rationalize his exploitation of his client by changing the client's mind with his psychological toolbox. The journalist also has a toolbox, but it is far more limited in scope.

A local journalist could play a significant role in his community by reporting on betrayed clients or legal system misconduct. Lawyers, however, have the power to stop journalists from reporting. The threat of legal action and the termination of access journalism, especially in smaller towns and cities, is often enough to keep legal system misconduct concealed.

In a case in Wisconsin, a client who wished to counter false information by hiring a public relations firm found it impossible to do so, due to the influence of his own lawyer. It emerged that using a PR firm necessitated revealing negligence on the part of the legal system in the PR firm's region. Agreeable at first, the PR firm asked for the name of the lawyer currently representing the client. The next day the firm declined the work without providing a reason. The client approached a second PR firm. The firm also asked for the name of the current lawyer. Again, the firm declined the work, no reason given. When the client questioned his lawyer about his involvement in the refusals, he smugly responded, "Did they tell you that I influenced them?"

Were a journalist to bypass the lawyer to approach his client directly, that journalist may find the door to future information closed by that lawyer or even his local tribe, depending on the rank of the lawyer in the hierarchy. A lawyer will be happy to provide exculpatory evidence on his client's behalf to a journalist, as long as that information is not too disruptive locally. A cost-benefit analysis takes place. If a client 'wins,' how does his victory impact the lawyer and his colleagues?

In both Switzerland and Wisconsin, many of the most serious claims made in this book and in *Beyond Outrage* regarding legal system failure and lawyer misconduct can be verified readily and simply by any journalist willing to look. Significant claims made here can indeed be found in public record, disclosed in official documents, even court and police documents. Journalists were informed over the years;

they have printed little. While verification is readily obtainable, the cost of such disclosure in terms of disrupted legal system players and institutions would be high, while many of these people are encountered at "train stations." Fortunately, the internet has changed the nature of the game.

Professional journalists and their personal/career interests are not as critical to exposing local legal wrongdoing today compared to a few years ago. While established media guarded the door to wide-spread exposure of legal wrongdoing in the past, journalists today must compete with citizen journalists or journalists more eager to fight the legal system (e.g. The Marshall Project (www.themarshallproject.org). This author, as one example, will promote the disclosure of legal system wrongdoing on the website www.lawyersbrokenbad.com. There should be an avenue for ordinary people to register their complaints about lawyers openly, bypassing self-serving, largely toothless lawyer oversight boards or feckless journalists and editors.

In the final analysis, justice in our legal system requires a thorough understanding of the true nature of the legal system. The cultural narrative of Legal System 1 is dangerously misleading; Legal System 2 thrives in common practice. An average lawyer will not engage fully in the defense of an average client; his relationship with a client will end long before his relationships with other, more influential lawyers, judges, police, and media in his professional circle do.

Typically, no single client can make a lawyer's career successful. The extent to which a lawyer defends his client in his local environment is a measure of his integrity; how he responds in practice to defend innocence against the headwinds of status quo bias is a measure of his courage. Trust is a weapon that a client hands his lawyer. It is not unreasonable to ask whether a lawyer will use that weapon against his own client.

PART 5

CHOOSING A 'GOOD' LAWYER

WE OFTEN HEAR patronizing, stock phrases such as "We believe in our legal system;" "Let the legal system do its job;" "The jury has spoken;" and "Our legal system works." from politicians and other influential voices. Indeed, our legal system can provide justice, but it fails too often. Success or failure depends on a courageous lawyer.

Considering the information presented in this book, focusing on choosing a 'good' lawyer by conventional means may be a poor approach to avoiding a bad lawyer. Instead, the better approach for an average client who wishes to proclaim innocence should be to think in terms of 'How can I ensure that my lawyer will apply Legal System 1?' This approach assumes that most law school graduates know the law as provided in Legal System 1. The problem for the average lawyer isn't that he is deficient at knowing theoretical law, but rather that he fails to apply it because he fears it implications. He spends too much time worrying about the effects of applying his knowledge in practice.

As implementing Legal System 1 fully can disadvantage a lawyer's career, a client does not actually hire a defense lawyer, he hires instead a *limited* defense lawyer. The limitations are variable depending on the legal context. Each client must individually evaluate the circumstances of power, politics, and influence within his community. In the process, he should come to understand the lawyer's vulnerabilities and therefore also his own when he hires the lawyer. The topic of the lawyer's interests in the community versus the client's, while possibly discomforting, should be discussed with a lawyer before legal representation.

While a client can come to understand that any lawyer faces pressure to avoid the exposure of negligence or wrongdoing in his community and to maintain his relationships, to favor settlements and to bow to local politics, the client must nevertheless demand that Legal System 1 have real meaning in his case. The lawyer must be made aware that he will be required to provide a vigorous defense and to carry out his professional responsibilities– just like practitioners in any other profession.

But how can this be brought about in practice?

Summarizing the information presented here, together with years of personal experience, I posit that the provision of false, intentionally misleading information by a lawyer to a client is the primary tool used by the bad lawyer to trap a client into paying for vigorous defense that the lawyer will ultimately try to avoid providing. In broad strokes, the lawyer wishes to retain a client, but then comes to fear confronting the legal system in the process of client defense. Any assurances provided to a client early on can mutate and be disavowed by the lawyer later, as readily as a change in the weather. The bad lawyer bridges the two imperatives in his professional life– hooking a client and avoiding various confrontations including a trial– by coercing a client to plea bargain and settle, a goal that he can attain unethically at little or no professional cost.

Every client should come to understand the concept of *limited* legal defense at the very start of lawyer representation. Success in legal representation as defined by a client is not the same as success as defined by the lawyer. Going to Google to search through 'good lawyers in your area' won't do it. The criteria for 'good' are too disparate between the lawyer and client. This is true of few if any other professions.

The primary reason why the tools of client betrayal can be used so readily in average legal cases is a lack of transparency, absence of meaningful oversight, and minimal or no interest on the part of the public and media. No one holds the lying lawyer responsible in average cases; the result therefore is a surfeit of lying lawyers. Only when 'lights are on and cameras are rolling' does a lawyer feel strongly compelled to follow Legal System 1. Lawyers tend to be different animals when their actions are being closely observed. Therefore, the issue of selecting a good lawyer becomes largely one of controlling the environment in which the lawyer works.

A lawyer is more likely to use Legal System 1 in a client's favor if the client, directly or subtly, can force the lawyer to make a cost-benefit analysis. The analysis must show him that deceiving his client will present career risks. If no one knows, cares, or believes that a client has been betrayed, the odds of client betrayal are greater. The more people who know that a client is being represented unethically, the greater the pressure on the lawyer to act ethically.

I once heard a notorious pedophile, who had remained hidden in the midst of elite society, describe the four words that he feared the most coming from a potential victim: "I'll tell my mommy." The same principle applies to bad lawyers. Poor representation and conduct shall not remain hidden. In practical terms, the client should garner direct, vocal support from as wide a circle of relatives, friends and supporters as possible. These supporters should ideally not be afraid to question or challenge the lawyer, having received client permission to do so. The more that trusted people protect and care openly for a lawyer's client, the better for the client.

Let the lawyer know that there is active interest in achieving justice and truth as advertised by Legal System 1. Bring along supporters to meetings with the lawyer. If he objects, ask him why. Compel him to explain why keeping his legal strategy concealed benefits you. Keep a diary of your conversations with the lawyer. Let him view that diary. Compel him to be continually aware of his promises and his pronouncements. If circumstances change, demand to know exactly why they have changed. If he claims to have found new evidence or witnesses, have him present those to you. Allow others to examine the evidence, letting the lawyer know you are doing so. The degree of comfort or discomfort exhibited through all of this by the lawyer will be an excellent indicator of his courage and intentions, honorable or not.

Lawyer coercion, just like coerced confessions in a police station, could become recognizable if an audio recording were available for all lawyer-client interactions. The disclosure of false promises, of the artificial induction of fear and guilt, and the use of emotional tools would eliminate an entire arsenal of weapons used against clients by their own lawyers. Full disclosure of the lawyer-client relationship would have the potential to turn around the dynamics of injustice, just as we have seen positive effect in the case of police with the use of cameras. To be sure, the average lawyer will display discomfort if a client asks to record their conversations. Nevertheless, the effort to do so will reveal a great deal about the lawyer, as the client provides his own test of the lawyer.

At the start of a legal representation a client asked his Swiss lawyer to permit his consultations with him to be audio recorded. The lawyer granted permission and a number of sessions were recorded. The circumstances changed when the client asked the lawyer to place specific misconduct by an influential lawyer, other persons of importance, and a court of first instance into an official legal appeal. Around that time the lawyer withdrew permission for recordings.

Asked to explain his withdrawal of consent, the lawyer had no clear response. He simply stated that he was no longer willing to be recorded. His consciousness of competing interests– his obligations to his client versus his loyalty to the legal tribe– caused him to re-examine his decision. But his new-found refusal served as a warning to his client. He understood at this point that he had hired a limited defense lawyer.

If a lawyer can be pressured to become a bad lawyer by a dysfunctional legal system, the reverse can also hold true. The safest way for a client to approach any lawyer is to have him understand from the start that his space will be private only to an extent determined by the client, and that the client is aware of the problem of lawyer betrayal, and why betrayal occurs.

There is only one set of rules that a lawyer should be proud to practice on behalf of an innocent client: that set of rules is called Legal System 1. Raising awareness of troublesome issues, emphasizing that a client will yell and scream if hurt, and using transparency to compel a lawyer to practice Legal System 1 is not an affront to a lawyer; it is a benefit–even if he doesn't know it at the time.

AFTERWORD

In Wisconsin, the *Milwaukee Journal-Sentinel* newspaper some years ago reported that a lawyer in that jurisdiction requested that a judge impose a remarkable penalty on an author: 400-million dollars. I was the author. I had dared expose local lawyers, police, and a judge in wrongdoing in essays. The lawyer claimed that such a high sum would entice a Swiss lawyer to stop the story told in the book *Beyond Outrage*. I was out of the country at the time and unrepresented in court. The judge denied the lawyer's absurd request, but then added the disturbing comment, "If I was convinced he had millions and millions of dollars, I would have."

The concept of freedom of speech suffered a hammer blow that day in Milwaukee, even though the 400-million dollar sum was rejected. Nevertheless, the highest penalty ever imposed against an author in Wisconsin was imposed against me— as of today over 1.5 million dollars.

How could a truthful narration concerning child abuse and poor lawyering in Milwaukee, as told in *Beyond Outrage*, justify any monetary penalty against an author, let alone a request for 400-million dollars? (An example of the type of informational essay that prompted this excess and panic among Milwaukee lawyers is presented in the Appendix.)

As is often the case, the word 'justify' has no practical meaning in the legal system because no one of significance dares ask probing questions. Bruised lawyer egos were enough justification to trash the First Amendment as far as the Milwaukee County legal jurisdiction was concerned. The point made by the judge and lawyers was: We are punishing an author for criticizing the legal system and exposing its faults.

Would there have been any monetary threshold to cause lawyers in Wisconsin to raise eyebrows or question the rationale or the fairness of asking for 400-million dollars? One billion dollars, for example? As time has gone by, however, I have come to welcome the notoriety; it is as clear a sign as any that Milwaukee lawyers had a lot to hide.

Lawyer wrath at what I wrote in *Beyond Outrage*– registering on their scale at 400- million dollars– did not end when I left the USA to live in Switzerland. Pressure from Wisconsin spilled over to Switzerland, ultimately leading to essays written there that exposed related, unethical lawyer conduct. That conduct included improper activities at a university where I taught, and questionable activities in scientific research and research papers that I edited, as well as shady activities by a Swiss professor of law. The essays, in turn, motivated the district attorney of the City of Basel to extend a warning to me about future publications on those subjects: "Don't do it!"

I was summoned to Basel police headquarters and there photographed and fingerprinted. My crime was that I continued to consider exposing wrongdoing in the legal system a justified endeavor for a writer. An assistant to the district attorney politely explained that publishing essays as I had been doing was, in any case, "having no effect." He had apparently not considered the irony that the district attorney's office was spending time and resources to stop essays that were "having no effect."

Both Milwaukee and Basel legal authorities could not handle written criticism that came their way without engaging in knee-jerk threats to stop the flow of information. Both jurisdictions overreacted; neither expecting the overreaction to receive any attention– the usual case for legal system misconduct when local media can be counted on to remain silent.

Both jurisdictions went beyond legal limits to conceal the use of Legal System 2. Their efforts to prevent written disclosure of wrongdoing demonstrate the human inclination to threaten the messenger. Happily, both jurisdictions also reinforce the conclusions concerning legal system failures arrived at in this book.

This book and *Beyond Outrage* should make clear the power of the pen over the sword. My writings about legal system corruption– in booklet-, essay- and book form extending over twenty years now– have brought about official reactions by the legal system that are astounding and very difficult to explain, unless the premises presented in this book are accepted as valid. Those reactions should also cause any reader to question our understanding of free speech and exactly what controls its limits– and it isn't 'truthfulness' or the lack thereof.

The fact that valid criticism, such as my writings, could work for the good of the community and spur change in the legal system– as it does in so many other areas– is subsumed by the legal system in the exigencies of ensuring that no one in the legal tribe is hurt or held responsible. We have seen the police as the obvious example of this, but that pattern of deflected responsibility pervades the entire legal system. Forced to choose between correction and concealment, the choice to conceal turns into a reflex in the legal system practically each time.

Regardless of the threats, writing and informing others of the dangers posed by the legal system is my personal resurrection from a grave Milwaukee lawyers started to dig for me, but never finished. The completion of this book therefore provides considerable, personal satisfaction.

It is too late for the knowledge presented in this book to help me. The most important legal case of my life was lost and is done and gone. The consequence of my failure to understand the real rules of the legal system in Milwaukee, Wisconsin will live inside me forever; I thereby lost my son.

If only one lawyer is encouraged to perform his professional duties with more integrity, or if one innocent client is influenced to hold his lawyer accountable, I will be pleased and rewarded by my efforts here.

Mark Inglin
Zermatt, Switzerland, 11/2016

APPENDIX

MISCELLANEOUS EXAMPLES OF LEGAL SYSTEM DYSFUNCTION
In researching this book I came upon many instances of legal system dysfunction. The examples that following further illustrate the points made in the preceding text.

The essay that follows is typical of the type of information that prompted the overreaction by Milwaukee lawyers, censoring this author. Note that real names were used in the original essays, while the names that follow in this essay are fictitious.

For more examples of legal system dysfunction, or to submit your own, please visit www.lawyersbrokenbad.com.

Corruption in the American Legal System
A sampling from the courthouse of Milwaukee, Wisconsin

Defense lawyer/judge/prosecutor exploit the stigma of mental illness to conceal legal wrongdoing at a trial

A trial that careened away from theoretical law into gross malfeasance took place in the Milwaukee County Courthouse. For lack of statistics, it is difficult to know just how unusual the trial was. The level of audacity on display, however, implied extraordinary confidence that few, if any, would question the misconduct.

Defense witnesses were intimidated and deliberately barred from testifying. All defense evidence was suppressed.

Jury selection excluded black Milwaukeeans. The prosecutor intentionally lied to the jury regarding police conduct, concealing critical, official and exculpatory court records. The prosecution presented its case last, an unprecedented deviation from the norm and proper form, but expedient to ensure a well-indoctrinated jury. The defense lawyer aided the prosecutor, betraying his own client during the proceedings, aiming a direct attack at him in his closing remarks. Perhaps most diabolical, however, was the insidious use of accusations of mental illness as a cover-up for the courtroom wrongdoing.

There had been no hint that the defendant suffered any form of psychological abnormality in the fourteen-month run-up to the trial. There was no history of adverse mental health. Indeed, in an official court record there stood a psychological evaluation not far in the past, stating that the defendant had been declared free of psychological abnormalities by a court-appointed psychologist in a divorce.

The judge, prosecutor and defense lawyer had good cause to undermine a defendant who had stubbornly refused to plea bargain and who had insisted on presenting exculpatory but embarrassing evidence at a trial. Earlier conduct by legal system players and law enforcement had not been exemplary; the defendant had taken note. The trial, the defendant expected, would allow favorable defense evidence to emerge. The judge, prosecutor and defense lawyer saw things otherwise.

Had the defendant undergone psychological evaluation in this case before trial, an official report devoid of negative psychological implications would have aided his defense, rendered his perceptions credible, and virtually assured acquittal. Under those circumstances, preprogramming the trial for a loss– a guilty verdict to protect colleagues– would have entailed high risk, as it would have eliminated the opportunity to undermine the credibility of the defendant in relation to his perception of reality after the trial.

No mention was therefore made of mental illness in advance of the trial. The circumstances changed in an instant, however, immediately following a guilty verdict.

Extensive misconduct at the trial was obfuscated by the judge in his pronouncements to the court in the form of an epiphany after the verdict; he expounded on what he now saw was "obvious mental frailty" on the part of the defendant: "Maybe he doesn't see it, but I do," while at the same time the prosecutor had worked the courtroom and, at sentencing, lectured the jury and others on the "obvious" nature of defendant's psychiatric problems, but also how "no other jurisdiction must be allowed to review this case."

What should have been "obvious" was the report of clean mental health that existed in the court record, and that any 'obvious' indications of mental health issues should have been addressed before the trial, not used as an excuse to explain bizarre procedural deviations after the trial. But a calculation was at work here: A man who has been denied justice in such a crude form and betrayed by his own defense lawyer is, indeed, likely to suffer considerable emotional pain. Such pain might then well be diagnosed by a therapist. Based on experience with defendants found guilty of crime, there was good reason to assume that a report of 'clinical depression' or a 'recommendation for medication' or some other psychological aberration would emerge in a following psychological report. It was thus important for the judge to order a post-trial psychological evaluation for a man now a criminal for the first time in his life, and who had suffered the shock of an un-American trial, including betrayal by his own lawyer.

The judge's subsequent instructions to the probation officer read, "This man belongs in a mental institution," an instruction that the probation office observed was the most unusual instruction that he had ever received from a judge.

The abrupt pivoting in the newly found awareness by judge and prosecutor betrayed an agenda intent on protecting the status quo. The lawyer for the appeal wanted no parts of examining the mental health issue, but he did promise to reveal the profound misconduct at trial, and to file for ineffective assistance of counsel. At the last minute– after being paid– he opted for grounds of legal technicalities, while the issues that would have implicated colleagues in misconduct– and protected his client– remained unexplored.

The story continues...

The return of the court-ordered mental health evaluation yielded bad news ...

Lawyer Bob Smith represented plaintiff/lawyer Jim Jones in a libel case that followed the trial. Jones was accused of ethical and legal violations at the trial in a series of booklets published locally by his former client. The law, had it been applied in straightforward fashion, would not have upheld lawyer Jones in this matter. Lawyer Smith therefore bypassed theoretical Legal System 1; he opted instead to use practical Legal System 2 to protect lawyer Jones.

Lawyer Joe Johnson represented Jones' former client, the author of the accusing booklets. One day he received a phone call: "You know, Joe," lawyer Smith implored with a dose of intimidation, "you should stop representing your client; he has– you know– certain ... mental problems."

Lawyer Smith was referring to the mental health report submitted to the Milwaukee court by psychologist Dr. Charlie Chase. In brief, the report stated that Chase had evaluated the author, concluding that his perception of reality was not accurate, i.e. psychosis. Furthermore, a second, earlier court-ordered evaluation by Dr. Sam Samson included a complaint by him that the booklet author had refused to take his medication.

The judge and prosecutor had both played amateur psychologists, and they had both won. The reports substantiated that lawyer Johnson's client was, indeed, not credible, which was the turning point in the libel case and reason to deny allegations of wrongful conduct at the trial.

It remains unclear how lawyer Smith availed himself of supposedly confidential mental health reports. What is clear is that his use of Legal System 2– as he bypassed the law on behalf of lawyer Jones– was very effective. From that time forward the author's claims against lawyer Jones fell on deaf ears– everywhere. Accusations merely turned into evidence of continued mental illness, as lawyers Smith and Jones gladly pointed out.

The damaging mental health reports followed the booklet author surreptitiously for years, impacting his life. They skewed critical decisions in a negative direction in a way that one would expect: mental illness in the form of psychosis renders an individual invisible and unheard.

The booklet author himself remained unaware of the damaging psychological reports making the rounds. Of course, he knew that both Drs. Chase and Samson had written favorable psychological evaluations, even a glowing report from Dr. Chase following the trial, implying that there might have been a problem with the legal system in which lawyer Jones operated. Chase's report had cast doubt on the truthfulness of lawyer Jones, but it had also done far more.

Dr. Chase's psychological evaluation was couched such that it conformed precisely to the requirements of Wisconsin law that would have guaranteed an acquittal for Jones' client, the defendant, at the trial– law that allows a father to protect a child who is in immanent danger. This fact was the focus of the earlier legal case. Had Chase's report been issued before the trial, it would have changed the outcome of guilty to a charge of interfering with child custody by 180 degrees, allowing a father to see his son again.

The judge, prosecutor and defense lawyer were well aware of how such a positive evaluation would have undermined their ability to conceal earlier legal system wrongdoing. The judge therefore waited to spring a trap that he and the prosecutor had good reason to believe could not have been sprung earlier. A guilty verdict after a bizarre, pre-programmed trial fit well with a defendant who was mentally ill. After taking that bold step and making that pronouncement, however, it became essential to maintain the fiction by any means.

There can be little doubt that lawyer Smith examined Dr. Chase's original, favorable report and recognized the inherent danger that it posed, as he was the reporter at large and loud mouthpiece for the fictitious evaluation. Mental illness was the attribute that kept criticism at bay and made some sense, and that kept lawyer Smith's cronies from accountability. So he pushed it hard.

One day, years after the discrediting phone call to lawyer Johnson by lawyer Smith, the booklet author was required to undergo another psychological evaluation, a third time by a third psychologist, on orders by a probation officer. The grounds for the evaluation were nebulous, but the insistence on doing so was adamant. The booklet author, it emerged, was intent on continuing to write and to tell his story, an unwelcome prospect.

"Why were you sent here?" the third psychologist asked when she met the author.

"I really don't know. I was instructed to do so," the author replied.

"Your past evaluations show no problems... no issues at all," the psychologist observed.

"Yes, I explained that to the probation officer," he agreed.

"But I did notice something odd," the therapist continued. "Your two previous evaluations in Milwaukee do not match the reports that were submitted to the court there. They state the opposite. Is that why the probation officer sent you here to me?"

It was during this evaluation that the booklet author discovered for the first time that his two earlier evaluations had been altered to state the opposite of the original reports, then submitted to the court as official.

The author was stunned. The third psychologist specifically pointed out the damaging discrepancies, highlighting the falsified texts in yellow marker. She stated that no further evaluation was necessary. That first consultation became her last. She sent her report directly to the probation officer, with an exact copy to the author.

The two earlier, original psychological evaluations intended for the Milwaukee court had been intercepted on their way to a federal judge, then "summarized" for him by Betty Bar, the federal probation officer. She had signed off on the fraudulent wording, e.g. as from "… perceives reality accurately" to "does not perceive reality accurately." And e.g. from no mention of "medication" in Samson's report to "does not take his medication" attributed to Dr. Samson.

Sunlight turned into darkest night with just a few words.

A lawyer who saw both sets of psychological evaluations, the original and the altered, commented, "Isn't it clever… the way they did this to you."

Yes, clever indeed.

The booklet author contacted Dr. Samson, informing him that his report to the court had been altered to state the opposite of his original report. He contemplated this information for a few moments, then observed that anyone could see that the report submitted to the court was not his report, regardless of the attribution.

"How so?" Dr. Samson was asked.

"Because, " he replied. "I have no power to prescribe medication or to require that a patient take medication. That's public record. I'm a psychologist, not a medical doctor. It's obvious that the report submitted to the court is a fraud."

Dr. Chase was also contacted. He admitted that his report had been falsified; he even allowed that it wasn't the first time such a thing had happened. When asked to come forward with his information on altered reports, however, he demurred, "I work for the county; I'm close to retirement; I'm sorry."

But he did return a copy of his original report, with his signature.

The author then contacted a psychologist on the ethics committee for the Wisconsin Psychological Association, Dr. Tom Bone. Bone listened intently and promised that he would investigate. Some time later he contacted the author and informed him that, "I asked around; it turns out that what you're telling me is impossible. A lawyer would have to be the greatest scoundrel to attempt such a thing. It can't be done."

The author responded by offering to provide the official court reports alongside the actual reports from the psychologists.

"It can't happen; it just can't happen," Dr. Bone insisted. I'm sorry. There is no more that I can do."

Dr. Bone refused to present the evidence to the ethics committee.

The probation officer who had demanded the third evaluation, Mr. Collin Watson of St. George, Utah, had been informed that earlier reports submitted to the court were frauds; he remained silent.

The judge in the case, Ralph Cramden, was informed of the falsified psychological reports. He sent the author a letter, stating that the issue "is no longer in my jurisdiction." No attempt was made to correct the reports. They remain official to this day.

When informed, fear on the parts of Drs. Chase and Bone had been palpable. The lawyers involved in the fraud had influence and mean reputations. Careers or worse would have been at stake. It was fear that kept exposure and criticism at bay.

Had Dr. Bone been capable of removing himself from the threat associated with the adverse circumstances, he would have recognized his reaction to be that of classic denial– just like they teach in psychology textbooks. Had the reporters who might have investigated the wrongful conduct examined their own behavior, they would have recognized the concept of "access journalism" and the power of status quo bias staring them in the face.

The evidence sits there for anyone to review, patient confidentiality not withstanding in this case. For the public records alone clash. Likely, based on Dr. Chase's pronouncement, there are other cases, too... possibly unknown to the victims.

The problem isn't finding the evidence; the problem is looking at the evidence and speaking up.

It speaks volumes that lawyer Smith had the confidence to exert influence on others using falsified mental health reports, reports that he theoretically had no right to access in the first place, let alone alter. But theoretical law played no role in this case. Legal System 2 was what mattered.

This is also one of many, routine cases where local media turned aside for the sake of future "access journalism," to ensure favor later, in more prominent cases. The legal authorities, meanwhile, have little incentive for "pulling on the thread," implicating colleagues in misconduct in a tight legal community.

Nota bene: As recently as the summer of 2016, lawyer Smith was still making use of his reference to the false information on mental illness that he had promoted so effectively, years ago.

Further examples:

Wisconsin: A young, criminal defense lawyer just starting out in practice listened as a private investigator described numerous professional violations by a well-established, local lawyer. The lawyer's failures resulted in the incarceration of his innocent client. "You already know," the lawyer informed the investigator, "that even though you can prove all of this, the regulatory board won't take any action against him; you already know that."

Switzerland: A Zurich lawyer advised his client that his rights had been seriously violated in a police interrogation. The client expected the information would benefit his defense, but the police were protecting an institution with influence in their community. The interests of the institution, in turn, were represented by a prominent law professor. The client's lawyer felt the pressure of legal system hierarchy. He severely self-limited his defense of the client, ultimately refusing to present evidence favorable to his client but damaging to the police and the institution.

Wisconsin: A criminal defense lawyer and a judge were professionally entangled and mutually dependent to the point where the lawyer often felt as ease to make facetious references and inappropriate jokes in open court. For example, the lawyer provided absurd reasons for postponing trial dates, including attending a golf outing held by the Make-a-Wish organization and the need to plan a vacation to France. When questioned in that judge's courtroom about why he improperly held 100,000 dollars in bail money in his private account rather than in the court bail account, the lawyer responded, "That's an old defense lawyer's trick," to laughter all around. The judge then suggested that the lawyer return the bail money to the client. The lawyer, however, subsequently simply refused to do so. When the judge was notified of this failure later, he stated that the lawyer had assured him, in court, that bail money "will be returned." But no date had been stipulated. One year later, the lawyer subtracted unapproved expenses from the bail funds, returning a diminished amount of money to his client.

Switzerland: A client sued a small-town business for improper dismissal from employment. Some days before a court hearing the lawyer for the company called the plaintiff's lawyer, threatening her physically if she carried out her plans to expose the company and defend her client. The judge found in plaintiff's favor for improper dismissal, but the threatening conduct by the company's lawyer went unexposed and was overlooked by the judge.

Wisconsin: An experienced criminal defense lawyer instructed his client to appear at an important meeting in court, in front of the judge. The appearance was claimed to be related to "evidence," but no further information was provided. The court appointment was for 10:00 AM. At about 10:15 AM, with no sign of the judge, the lawyer left the courtroom and returned with a document that he said was "urgent" and required the client's signature. The document comprised several pages filled with legalese, but on page three one provision stuck out. By signing the document the client would have relinquished his claim of innocence, diametrically opposed to his precise instructions to his lawyer. The lawyer had hoped for reflexive acquiescence to lawyer instruction, which worked often enough to justify staging deceitful theater. The sole purpose of the courtroom meeting was to create tension intended to lead the client to sign-away his right to a trial.

New Zealand: A New Zealand prosecutor explained that a defendant loses his identity to that of his defense lawyer, who is the enemy. He put forth that a victory over the defense lawyer was what mattered to him and what motivated him and his entire office. The "truth" of any particular case, he explained, is defined as the outcome to a trial at that very specific time of the trial and under those specific circumstances. Later, there may be another 'truth,' e.g. the defendant was not actually guilty, "but that truth belongs in another setting and another time, not in my setting and not in time at trial. At trial," he went on the explain, "a prosecutor demonstrates fitness or lack of fitness versus a defense lawyer, not his client." That the state itself found the outcome to this contest the determining factor in a defendant's future was not a matter for the prosecutor's consideration. He shared no responsibility in a case in which a defendant was found guilty because of ineffective assistance of counsel.

Wisconsin: A lawyer used falsified mental health reports to mislead another defense lawyer into thinking that his client suffered from psychosis, thereby undermining his trust in his client's pronouncements. The false report was then submitted to and accepted by a judge as official. As psychological reports are theoretically highly confidential, it is difficult– but not impossible with a patient's permission– to compare an actual report to a falsified, official report. This, however, requires cooperation, effort, and a willingness to disclose wrongdoing if discovered.

Switzerland: A law professor at a Swiss university represented three fellow professors against a criminal accusation, but with conflict of interest looming. The opposing lawyer in the case informed his client that the possible conflict of interest rendered the professor's representation of the three defendants clearly legally unethical. "No ordinary lawyer could do this," he explained, "but he will not be held accountable by the professional oversight board because he is well known and influential." A second lawyer, acknowledging the same unethical conduct by the professor, also refrained from challenging the law professor or using the information to aid his own client.

Wisconsin: A highly experienced criminal defense lawyer made a point of sending personal letters to clients of colleagues after they had been sentenced by the court. The letters assured them that they had received top-class representation by their lawyer, regardless of the outcome. The lawyer emphasized in these letters how much worse the outcome could have been (the threat made to gain a plea bargain, for example), and how effective their defense had been. In turn, the same was done for him by his colleagues. "The game," the lawyer explained, "is one of expectations." Moreover, if a client complained to the regulatory board about poor defense by his lawyer, such letters constituted evidence to the board, confirming that another legal expert had appraised the initial defense as outstanding.

Switzerland: After two years of preparation for a trial and the collection of extensive exculpatory evidence, a client was threatened by his own lawyer with undefined "punishment" if he did not settle the case out of court. This was followed by the lawyer's refusal to continue representation, as the evidence was not 'clean;' it implicated colleagues in wrongdoing.

Wisconsin: In spite of effusive promises of vigorous defense initially, a Wisconsin lawyer just starting out in practice began threatened his clients with refusal to continue representation if they avoided his settlement agreements. He had learned from older colleagues in the firm that such threats caused client panic and he considered the threats to be standard legal practice.

Switzerland: An experienced defense lawyer familiar with the legal systems in Switzerland and the USA admitted that circumstances in the legal system in Switzerland were even worse than in the USA. The problem, he carefully explained, had to do with excessive prosecutorial power in Switzerland. He himself, however, shied well away from exposing what he openly considered a bad system, but only in safe circles. He was able to earn a good living by practicing his profession right up to the point of conflict with the prosecution, at which time he would yield and force a settlement on the client, whom he characterized as the "weakest link."

Wisconsin: When challenged by clients regarding the quality of his representation, a lawyer repeatedly made use of intimidation in the form of letters suggesting that the client must have been confused by stress or, worse, that the client was mentally imbalanced. As was common with his colleagues, he took advantage of stressful conditions imposed on a client by the legal system to absolve himself of responsibility (the client is imagining things) as he attempted to undermine the client's confidence in his own perceptions.

Switzerland: A false accusation in violation of due process was put forth by members of an influential institution against an employee. A criminal complaint aimed at the institution followed, leading to embarrassment for the instigators of the false accusation. The evidence of misconduct that led to the false accusation was incontrovertible and widely known. Against this evidence, a district attorney simply put forth a unilateral, written declaration: the incident of false accusation had, in fact, never occurred. There had been no pretense of subtlety in this decree; it was the straightforward refutation of documented history and evidence, practicable by the misuse of the power of the office to protect the status quo, along with the confidence that local media would fail to report the incident.

Wisconsin: A lawyer explained to a potential client who was unfamiliar with the legal system that he could not get him into court for four weeks on an initial hearing of his case. The client phoned another lawyer, who replied with requisite gravity that the client's situation was critical, and that he would immediately request a court hearing. The client naturally chose the second lawyer. The court hearing took place six weeks later.

Switzerland: A client specifically requested of his lawyer that he be given adequate time to consider and reflect on all decisions in his case. The lawyer agreed to do so, yet repeatedly presented his client with decisions that he claimed needed to be made immediately. These were accompanied by excuses such as: "I'm sorry, I was sick"; "I'm sorry, we are just heading on vacation... I need to know your decision right now"; "I'm sorry, I was so overworked that I had no chance to get to it until now. It won't happen again." This lawyer was typical in that he had learned that deadline stresses ultimately lead to client frustration and anger, and to decisions more favorable to the lawyer's needs.

Wisconsin: During a deposition, but off the record, the opposing lawyer asked the plaintiff what his demands were for settlement of the case. The plaintiff answered, "I want the truth to emerge concerning the rigged trial and serious misconduct by the defense lawyer." "That," the lawyer replied confidently, "will never happen."

Switzerland: A lawyer agreed in advance to charge 250 Swiss francs to write a letter for a client. When the bill arrived, it was more than double the agreed amount. The client objected. The lawyer insisted she needed more money for her effort, but had not informed the client. The lawyer then attempted by legal means to collect her extra fee. Fortunately, the legal means included allowing the right of formal objection, including providing reasoning. The client wrote that the extra billing was a "fraudulent attempt to collect more money than had been agreed upon." The lawyer stopped her demands and was never heard from again.

Wisconsin: A highly regarded criminal defense lawyer was convinced of his client's innocence, yet applied psychological pressure on the client to plea bargain. Forced at one point to explain to his client why he kept postponing trial dates, the collection of vital evidence, and testimonials when the odds were well in favor of acquittal, the lawyer blurted out in anger, "Don't think for one minute that I will feel guilty if you lose. I go home; you go to prison." The motivation for the plea bargain had been the lawyer's own fears of losing at trial, while the client had long been at peace with his decision to go to trial.

Wisconsin: A defense lawyer and long-time fixture in his local legal establishment could not dissuade his client from insisting on a trial in a third-degree felony case. The client, a low-profile individual ignored by media, had steadily maintained his innocence over many months, while the available evidence strongly supported his claim. However, the case involved earlier misconduct by police and lawyers vital to the defense. The defense lawyer deliberately failed to hand in a witness list to the court before the deadline. He intimidated defense witnesses who appeared at court by implying that certain aspects of their histories represented vulnerabilities and might need to be explored on the witness stand. The defense lawyer sabotaged his own client by losing at a trial with an outcome that he considered of little consequence to his career, but that would spare his future relationships within his legal community.

The lawyer for the appeal, a lawyer in the same town, roared outrage when he examined the trial transcript and the overt misconduct. He promised exposure and a legal complaint for ineffective assistance of counsel. In the course of representation, however, the appellate lawyer simply broke his promise and, contrary to the client's emphatic instructions, focused on minor technical issues. The client lost the appeal and the wrongdoing was covered up permanently.

BIBLIOGRAPHY

BOOKS:

With Justice for None: Destroying an American Myth. Gerry Spence. 1989, Crown Publishers, Random House, New York, NY;

Battle for the Mind: A Physiology of Conversion and Brainwashing. William Sargant. first published 1957 by ISHK, Los Altos CA;

Thinking Fast and Slow: Daniel Kahnemann. 2011, Penguin Books, London, England;

The Defense is Ready: Life in the Trenches of Criminal Law. Leslie Abramson. 1997, Simon and Schuster, New York, NY;

The Varieties of Religious Experience: William James. Longman, 1902, London, England;

Just Mercy: A Story of Justice and Redemption. Bryan Stevenson. 2014, Spiegel and Grau, New York, NY;

Trauma and Cognitive Science: A Meeting of Minds, Science, and Human Experience. Freyd, J.J. and DePrince, A.P. Published as a special issue of the *Journal of Aggression,*

Maltreatment, & Trauma and as a book. 2001, Haworth Press, Philadelphia, PA;

The Power Paradox: How We Gain and Lose Influence. Dach Keltner. 2016, Penguin Press, London, England;

The Journalist and The Murderer. Janet Malcolm. 2004, Granta Books, London, England;

10-10-10: Suzy Welch, 2009, Scribner, New York, NY;

Beyond Outrage: Mark Inglin, 2011, available on Amazon.

ABOUT THE AUTHOR

Mark Inglin is a biologist, translator and editor. He has taught science and conducted research at the University of Wisconsin, operated a translation and editing service and, most recently, taught scientific writing at the University of Basel, Switzerland. He has also spent the last 20 years exposing corruption in the legal system and currently continues to edit science research publications.

This is the author's second book. The first, *Beyond Outrage* (www.beyond-outrage.com), describes personal experiences in the American legal system in a failed attempt to protect his son from abuse against the wishes of a corrupt legal establishment in Milwaukee.

www.ingramcontent.com/pod-product-compliance
Lightning Source LLC
Chambersburg PA
CBHW021406170526
45164CB00002B/526